THE
DYNAMIC
Difference

THE
DYNAMIC
Difference

DAVID HOCKING

HARVEST HOUSE PUBLISHERS
Eugene, Oregon 97402

THE DYNAMIC DIFFERENCE

Copyright © 1985 by David Hocking
Published by Harvest House Publishers
Eugene, Oregon 97402
(Formerly titled *Are You Spirit-Filled?*)

Library of Congress Catalog Card Number 85-061076
ISBN 0-89081-725-1

Printed in the United States of America.

To charismatics and noncharismatics
everywhere: May God help us
to love one another
in spite of our differences.

FOREWORD

*I have filled him with the Spirit of God, in
wisdom, in understanding, in knowledge, and
in all manner of workmanship (Exodus 31:3).*

These words, spoken by God to Moses, concerned
the work of an artist named Bezaleel during the building
of a tabernacle. Because Bezaleel had been filled with
the Holy Spirit, he was enabled to create beautiful
designs for the tabernacle in not just one kind of craftsmanship but in many. Bezaleel was *dynamically* different.

In the book of Judges we learn that the Holy Spirit
came upon people to give them special ability. Consider the following passages:

Judges 3:10—"The Spirit of the Lord came
upon him [Othniel]."

Judges 6:34—"The Spirit of the Lord came
upon Gideon."

Judges 11:29—"The Spirit of the Lord came
upon Jephthah."

Judges 14:6—"The Spirit of the Lord came
mightily upon him [Samson—cf.14:19;
15:14]."

While these passages do not explicitly say that these
leaders were "filled with the Holy Spirit," it would be
difficult to argue that they were not.

First Samuel 11:6 says of Saul, "The Spirit of God
came upon Saul." But in 1 Samuel 16:14 we read,
"The Spirit of the Lord departed from Saul." Again,

1 Samuel 16:13 says of David, "The Spirit of the Lord came upon David from that day forward." But in Psalm 51:11 David prayed, "Do not take Your Holy Spirit from me." In Old Testament times, it appears that the Holy Spirit both "came upon" believers and "departed from" them.

Over the years, the term "Spirit-filled," like "born again," has been stripped of its importance and meaning through overuse and misapplication. That's unfortunate, because both are powerful terms.

When someone says "I'm a born-again Christian," he speaks redundantly. All Christians are born-again, or else they are not Christians at all. The term "born-again" speaks of the spiritual birth which makes us Christians. It happens the moment we believe in the death and resurrection of Jesus Christ and receive Him as our Lord and Savior.

To be "Spirit-filled" is another matter. It is not a special experience for a select few. We're not talking here about "supersaints" or unusually gifted individuals. Being filled with the Holy Spirit is available to all believers and is essential to living the Christian life the way it was meant to be lived.

Two problems confront us:

1. *A problem of knowledge:* dealing with the identity, personality, and work of the Holy Spirit.

2. *A problem of application:* dealing with our response to what we know about the Holy Spirit.

The first problem is confusing because Christians disagree on what the Bible actually teaches about the Holy Spirit. The second problem is disturbing because it depends so heavily upon the first problem and demands some intellectual honesty and humility—something most of us do not have in great abundance!

It is possible to be a Christian but not be "Spirit-filled." The Bible describes such a believer as "carnal." The normal Christian life is one that is filled with the Holy Spirit. God never encourages believers to be carnal. In fact, we are frequently warned about the dangers of carnality.

Because the Holy Spirit makes the *dynamic* difference in every believer's life, it is my hope and prayer that you will be lead into a deeper understanding of the vital relationship possible with the Holy Spirit of God.

CONTENTS

1. Who Is The Holy Spirit? 13

2. What Happened On The Day Of
   Pentecost? 31

3. Are You Baptized With The Spirit? 55

4. What About Spiritual Gifts? 75

5. Are Tongues The Proof? 95

6. Should We Speak In Tongues? 111

7. Are Tongues For Today? 125

8. What Hinders The Spirit? 143

9. Why Do We Need The Holy Spirit? 157

10. Can We Know If We Are Spirit-Filled? 173

1

Who Is The Holy Spirit?

One pastor in the Midwest told me at a large Bible conference where I was speaking that he is afraid to speak about the Holy Spirit because it is such a controversial subject in his church. How sad!

Many religions speak of the Holy Spirit as though He were an "it." They speak of Him as though He were merely a force or an influence from God. But the Bible teaches two important facts about the Holy Spirit:

1. The Holy Spirit is God.
2. The Holy Spirit is a real Person.

The Spirit of God is not simply a part of God; He is actually God! He is a real Person, possessing all the marks of personality that any one of us has.

When we speak of being filled with the Holy Spirit we are not simply dealing with a religious experience. The Spirit-filled life is not a spiritual hypodermic needle that gives us a shot of spiritual power every now and then; we're talking about having the God who made us coming into our lives and filling us with His presence.

13

What an awesome thought! Too many believers speak only of an experience, and fail to sense that a real Person has come to share our lives with us.

The Holy Spirit Is God!

The word "trinity" does not appear in the Bible, but the Bible presents three Persons as one God. God is not three gods. He is one God, but He manifests Himself in three separate and distinct Personalities—the Father, the Son, and the Holy Spirit.

Let's take a closer look at the biblical facts that affect our view about the deity of the Holy Spirit.

1. *The Holy Spirit is called God in Acts 5:3,4.*

This story deals with Peter's confrontation of Ananias and Sapphira, who lied about some land they had sold. In Acts 5:3 Peter says:

> Ananias, why has Satan filled your heart to lie *to the Holy Spirit?*

In verse 4 he says:

> You have not lied to men but *to God.*

The two statements are parallel. The Holy Spirit is obviously called God in this passage.

2. *The Holy Spirit does work that only God can do.*

Only God can create, yet the Holy Spirit was involved in the creation of the universe and mankind. Genesis 1:2 says that "the Spirit of God was hovering over the face of the waters." Job 26:13 states, "By His Spirit He adorned the heavens." The Spirit of God was the One who beautified the universe as a painter or sculptor would do.

In Genesis 2:7 we learn of the Spirit's involvement with the creation of human life. It reads:

> The Lord God formed man of the dust of
> the ground, and breathed into his nostrils the
> breath of life; and man became a living being.

Job 33:4 adds, "The Spirit of God has made me, and the breath of the Almighty gives me life." The word "breath" in Genesis 2:7 and Job 33:4 is the same word "Spirit."

According to John 1:12,13, spiritual birth is the work of God. Yet in John 3:5 Jesus spoke of being "born of the Spirit." The apostle Paul referred to the "regeneration and renewing of the Holy Spirit" in Titus 3:5. Obviously, the Holy Spirit can do what only God can do. What other conclusions can we draw from this evidence but that the Holy Spirit is God?

3. *The Holy Spirit possesses divine attributes.*

The Bible speaks of the Holy Spirit's abilities in terms that can refer only to God. He is called the "eternal Spirit" in Hebrews 9:14. Obviously, only God is eternal; every other creature is limited by time. The Holy Spirit is described as being omnipresent (everywhere at once) in Psalm 139:7-10:

> Where can I go from Your Spirit? Or where
> can I flee from Your presence? If I ascend into
> heaven, You are there; if I make my bed in
> hell, behold, You are there. If I take the wings
> of the morning, and dwell in the uttermost
> parts of the sea, even there Your hand shall
> lead, and Your right hand shall hold me.

The Holy Spirit knows what God knows. First Corinthians 2:11 says: "No one knows the things of God except the Spirit of God." If He knows the things of God, then is He not also God?

He has the power to raise the dead, according to Romans 8:11. Such power is the possession of God. Is He not therefore omnipotent (all-powerful)?

These attributes (eternity, omnipresence, omniscience, omnipotence) belong to God, and the Bible assigns them to the Holy Spirit as well as to God the Father.

4. *The Holy Spirit is placed in positions of equality with God the Father.*

While this point is not overwhelming in terms of the evidence for the deity of the Holy Spirit, it is certainly part of the argument. In Matthew 28:19 our Lord commanded us to baptize people "in the name (singular) of the Father and of the Son and of the Holy Spirit." The word "name" in the singular suggests one God in three Persons.

Second Corinthians 13:14 is a final benediction or salutation to Paul's letter. It says:

> The grace of the Lord Jesus Christ, and the
> love of God, and the communion of the Holy
> Spirit be with you all. Amen.

The verse suggests a certain equality between the Father, Son, and Holy Spirit.

Believing that the Holy Spirit is the eternal God has tremendous importance to the believer who desires to be filled with the Holy Spirit. We are not talking about a mere influence or experience. The Holy Spirit is called God, He does the work that only God can do, He possesses divine attributes, and He is placed in positions of equality with God the Father. We can conclude only one thing: *The Holy Spirit is God!*

The person in my office seemed excited to share his experience with me. He said he had come into a new awareness of the Holy Spirit in his life. When I asked him about it, he spoke of feeling dizzy and experiencing chills all over his body. He said that some strange words flowed out of his mouth which he did not understand, but ones which he was sure came from God. He concluded that the experience was the filling of the Holy Spirit. The longer we talked, the more doubtful I was of his claim. He proceeded to tell me that God spoke to him directly. However, what he said he was told was contradictory to biblical teaching about God and His purposes and will. When I tried to explain that the Holy Spirit was God and would not direct him to violate the Word of God, he became defensive and argumentative.

It was sad indeed to find this man reluctant to learn that the Holy Spirit is God Himself, not simply an experience from God. I wonder how many people are confused about this most important matter.

What Difference Does It Make?

Plenty! If the filling of the Holy Spirit means that we are filled with God Himself, it puts a new light on everything we say and do. Our actions would reflect the character of God and demonstrate our allegiance to Him. What we say would conform to His Word. What we believe about ourselves would tend to glorify God more if we understood that the power and controlling factor in the Christian life is God, not simply an experience that we may have had.

Experiences are simply that—experiences. You may sincerely believe that your experiences are valid, but that is no guarantee that they actually are valid simply because you believe they are!

When a certain lady told me about her divorce and

remarriage, I was immediately aware that she had violated the teaching of the Bible. She had no justifiable reasons for what she did. All she claimed was that the Holy Spirit was leading her. She said she was Spirit-filled. I did not agree. Needless to say, my ability to counsel her immediately ceased. She said that I had no right to question her decision because she was filled with the Spirit.

How easily we can convince ourselves that the Spirit of God is leading us to do something when in reality it is simply our own desire! God does not contradict Himself. When you are filled with the Holy Spirit, your words and conduct will conform to the character and purposes of God, no matter what experience you may claim to receive.

When you are filled with the Holy Spirit, the God who made you controls your life. The eternal God has come to fill a creature of time—what a mystery and blessing that thought is! When God the Holy Spirit fills you, there are resources available to you that you would not otherwise have. His power knows no limit, and He has complete knowledge of all that lies ahead. It can be a marvelous experience to trust One who possesses all the attributes of the living God. It is certainly a miracle that the infinite God can localize Himself enough to dwell in our finite bodies. What a wonder!

Really a Person!

As I spoke of the personality of the Holy Spirit to a troubled lady who was frustrated by many disappointments in her life, tears came to her eyes. She said, "I can hardly believe what you're saying!" She seemed surprised to learn that the Bible presents the Holy Spirit as a real Person and that she could have a personal relationship with Him as she did with any other person. She was lonely, and to learn of the comforting presence of the Holy Spirit was indeed exciting to her. Though a Christian for many years, for some reason the thought of the personality of the Spirit had escaped her.

What do *you* believe about the Holy Spirit? Do you relate to Him as a real Person, or is He merely an influence or power to you? Consider these marks of personality which the Bible teaches belong to the Holy Spirit of God.

1. *Personal pronouns are used when referring to the Holy Spirit.*

In John 14:16,17 this fact is quite obvious:

> I will pray the Father, and He will give you another Helper, that *He* may abide with you forever, even the Spirit of truth, *whom* the world cannot receive, because it neither sees *Him* nor knows *Him*; but you know *Him*, for *He* dwells with you and will be in you.

Another passage that uses personal pronouns of the Holy Spirit, indicating that He is a real Person and not simply an "it," is John 16:7-15:

> I tell you the truth. It is to your advantage that I go away; for if I do not go away, the Helper will not come to you; but if I depart, I will send *Him* to you. And when *He* has come, *He* will convict the world of sin, and of righteousness, and of judgment: of sin, because they do not believe in Me; of righteousness, because I go to My Father and you see Me no more; of judgment, because the ruler of this world is judged. I still have many things to say to you, but you cannot bear them now. However, when *He*, the Spirit of

truth, has come, *He* will guide you into all truth; for *He* will not speak on *His* own authority, but whatever *He* hears *He* will speak; and *He* will tell you things to come. *He* will glorify Me, for *He* will take of what is Mine and declare it to you. All things that the Father has are Mine. Therefore I said that *He* will take of Mine and declare it to you.

There is no doubt about the use of these pronouns; they clearly identify the Holy Spirit as a Person.

2. *The Holy Spirit possesses intelligence.*

As mentioned earlier, 1 Corinthians 2:11 says that the Holy Spirit "knows" the things of God. Romans 8:27 adds these important words:

He who searches the hearts knows what the mind of the Spirit is, because He makes intercession for the saints according to the will of God.

Possessing a "mind" is a fundamental requirement of a personality. Isaiah 11:2 gives these mental capacities to the Holy Spirit:

The Spirit of wisdom and understanding
The Spirit of counsel
The Spirit of knowledge

My ability to understand and know things exists because I have been made in the image of God and after His likeness. My capacity to reason and to plan for the future comes from God Himself. The Holy Spirit is God, and since we have been made in the image of God, there is something about the Holy Spirit that is similar to ourselves: We are both personalities with the ability to think, plan, reason, understand, and analyze. We have a mind because God has a mind.

3. *The Holy Spirit has a will.*

Human beings are distinguished from animals by *volitional response* (as opposed to mere instinctive reactions to the stimuli of the immediate environment). Animals are not directed by a will in the classic sense of that word. They respond to the situation and the environment around them. I can will to do things that have not yet occurred but exist only in the deep recesses of my mind. Animals cannot. Animals, therefore, are not persons, though they seem at times to manifest certain traits of personality.

First Corinthians 12:11 says that the Holy Spirit distributes spiritual gifts to each believer "as He wills." He makes the decision as to which believer gets what gifts.

Second Peter 1:20,21 states:

> Knowing this first, that no prophecy of the Scripture is of any private interpretation, for prophecy never came by the will of man, but holy men of God spoke as they were moved by the Holy Spirit.

The Bible is not the product of the human will. The writers of Scripture were guided by the will of the Holy Spirit so that what was written was guaranteed to be reliable and accurate.

4. *The Holy Spirit manifests emotional responses.*

Emotion is one of the marks of personality with which we all identify readily. We feel things even when there is no reason to do so. We can feel sad or lonely when surrounded by people who have given us no cause to feel such emotions. We can get angry at people who have done nothing against us and with whom we have no personal relationship.

When we speak of the emotions of the Holy Spirit, it is indeed encouraging to learn from the Bible that He experiences responses similar to ours. Because He is a Person, He has emotions. For example, Ephesians 4:30 says that He can be grieved. Romans 5:5 says that He loves. He also "lusts" against our sinful desires (called the "flesh"), according to Galatians 5:17. James 4:5 teaches that He "yearns jealously" over us because He dwells within us.

Hebrews 10:29 reveals that the Holy Spirit can be insulted, and Acts 7:51 adds that He can be resisted. The Holy Spirit is a real Person with feelings and responses just like we have!

Symbols of the Spirit

In continuing to identify the person and work of the Holy Spirit, let us take a brief look at the symbols which are used in the Bible to describe Him.

1. The symbol of fire.

It is common to see a flame used to symbolize the work of the Holy Spirit. Two passages of Scripture are usually used to illustrate the Holy Spirit as "fire." One is Acts 2:3, which describes the event on the Jewish festival of Pentecost when "tongues, as of fire" appeared in the upper room where 120 believers were gathered. Acts 2:4 says, "They were all filled with the Holy Spirit." The symbol of fire is used to indicate the person and work of the Holy Spirit of God.

A second passage is found in Matthew 3:11,12, where John the Baptist says:

> I indeed baptize you with water unto repentance, but He who is coming after me is mightier than I, whose sandals I am not worthy to carry. He will baptize you with the Holy Spirit and fire. His winnowing fan is in His hand, and He will thoroughly purge His threshing floor, and gather His wheat into the barn; but He will burn up the chaff with unquenchable fire.

John baptizes with water, but Jesus baptizes with the Holy Spirit and fire. The baptism of the Holy Spirit is for believers, but the baptism of fire is for unbelievers. The chaff represents unbelievers and is burned up with unquenchable fire. The wheat which is gathered into the barn represents believers, who will be baptized with the Holy Spirit.

Fire can represent power as well as purification when it is used as a symbol of the Holy Spirit.

2. *The symbol of a dove.*

When Jesus was baptized by John the Baptist in the Jordan River, the Holy Spirit's presence was manifested in an unusual way. Consider the Gospel accounts carefully:

> Matthew 3:16—"He saw the Spirit of God descending like a dove and alighting upon Him."
> Mark 1:10—"He saw the heavens parting and the Spirit descending upon Him like a dove."
> Luke 3:22—"The Holy Spirit descended

in bodily form like a dove upon Him."
    John 1:32—"I saw the Spirit descending
from heaven like a dove, and He remained
upon Him."

In each case we read that the Holy Spirit descended. In each case it says "like a dove." Once (Luke 3:22) it describes the descent as being "in bodily form like a dove." It does not say that the Holy Spirit *is* a dove, but merely that His descent was *similar to* a dove's descent.

The descent of a dove is gentle and beautiful, often a symbol of peace and tranquility. It is quite the opposite of violence or attack.

While the fire may picture power and purification, the dove pictures peace and quiet.

In the Song of Solomon, Solomon says of his lover, "You have dove's eyes" (4:1). One of the interesting facts about a dove is that it is loyal to its mate all its life! Solomon saw loyalty in his beloved's eyes. The Spirit of God will be faithful and loyal to us. It also pictures the purity of the Spirit, for there is no unfaithfulness in His character. Jesus said in Matthew 10:16 that we are to be "harmless as doves." The word "harmless" means "unmixed" or "innocent"—no ulterior motives or hypocrisy. The common adjective used of the Spirit of God is the word "holy." He is the *Holy* Spirit!

When the descent of the Holy Spirit is described in the Gospel accounts, it is interesting to observe these words:

    Matthew says, "alighting upon Him."
    John says, "He remained upon Him."

The dove is a trusting bird, and yet no bird is more easily frightened. The dove is mentioned about 50 times in the Bible, with many references to its use as a sacrificial animal. When caged, it was usually quite docile.

"Fire" and "dove"—what fascinating symbols of the Holy Spirit of God in terms of His attributes and work!

3. *The symbol of wind.*

The word "Spirit" can also be translated "wind" or "breath." When the Spirit of God came on the day of Pentecost, the Bible speaks of "a sound from heaven, as of a rushing mighty wind, and it filled the whole house where they were sitting" (Acts 2:2). This kind of wind produces a powerful noise and represents great power.

Jesus spoke of the Spirit's work in John 3:8 and compared it to the wind:

> The wind blows where it wishes, and you
> hear the sound of it, but cannot tell where it
> comes from and where it goes. So is every-
> one who is born of the Spirit.

The wind cannot be seen, and in that respect is a subtle reminder that the work of the Holy Spirit is invisible. Because the wind "blows where it wishes" to blow, and we can't tell where it comes from or where it is going, we have a picture of the sovereignty of the Holy Spirit's work. He works in ways that we do not understand and performs things on His own time schedule, not ours!

"Fire," "dove," and "wind"—these are wonderful symbols of the Holy Spirit and the way He works, giving us much insight into His personality and power.

4. *The symbol of water.*

According to John 7:2 and 7:14, Jesus attended one of the Jewish festivals called Succoth, or Tabernacles. It commemorated the time of Israel's wanderings in the wilderness, when they lived in temporary dwellings. During that time of difficulty and trial, God provided for His people in a most spectacular way. In addition to bringing bread from heaven (called "manna"), He also supplied water out of a rock. In honor of that event when the water came out of a rock, the priests poured out water from the golden vessels of the temple on the last day of the feast. John 7: 37-39 records the unusual actions of Jesus at that moment:

> On the last day, that great day of the feast, Jesus stood and cried out, saying, "If anyone thirsts, let him come to Me and drink. He who believes in Me, as the Scripture has said, out of his heart will flow rivers of living water." But this He spoke concerning the Spirit, whom those believing in Him would receive; for the Holy Spirit was not yet given, because Jesus was not yet glorified.

Paul wrote in 1 Corinthians 10:4:

> [They] all drank the same spiritual drink. For they drank of that spiritual Rock that followed them, and that Rock was Christ.

The symbolism involves the following:

Rock = Christ
Water = Spirit

Jesus described the ministry of the Holy Spirit like an artesian well, with "rivers of living water." When the Holy Spirit is given, eternal life is given. A person receives the Spirit when he believes on Jesus Christ, the Rock out of which the water came.

A Quick Summary

The Holy Spirit is described by the following symbols:

Fire: symbolizing His power and His purification of the believer.
Dove: symbolizing His purity and peace-
fulness.
Wind: symbolizing His power, sovereignty,
and invisible work.
Water: symbolizing His eternal life, which He
gives to all who believe in Jesus
Christ.

5. *The symbol of clothing.*

In His instructions to His disciples after His resurrection, Jesus said (Luke 24:49):

Behold, I send the Promise of My Father
upon you; but tarry in the city of Jerusalem
until you are endued with power from on
high.

The word "endued" means to put clothes on. Jesus
wanted us to understand our need of being clothed with
the Holy Spirit. The idea is that of protection which our
clothing brings to our nakedness, or it might refer to the
matter of our righteousness and godly lifestyle. Ephesians 4:24 tells us to "put on the new man which was
created according to God, in righteousness and true
holiness." To "put on" is referring to the act of getting
dressed. Since He is the *Holy* Spirit, the idea of our
holiness is certainly appropriate to this symbolism of
being clothed with the Holy Spirit.

However, the primary point which Jesus made about
being clothed with the Spirit deals with power for our

witnessing, perhaps in the sense of being prepared or ready. We might say "dressed for the occasion." When we witness for the Lord, we need to be dressed properly with the clothing of the Holy Spirit of God.

6. *The symbol of oil.*

Acts 10:38 presents this symbol of the Spirit's ministry in the life of Jesus:

> God anointed Jesus of Nazareth with the Holy Spirit and with power, who went about doing good and healing all who were oppressed by the devil, for God was with Him.

The anointing oil represents the approval and choice of God. Jesus is the Messiah, and this means that He is the Anointed One of God, uniquely selected by God for His special purpose. In Isaiah 61:1 the Servant of the Lord, the Messiah, says:

> The Spirit of the Lord God is upon Me, because the Lord has anointed Me.

Paul connects the anointing of God with the work of the Holy Spirit in 2 Corinthians 1:21,22:

> He who establishes us with you in Christ and has anointed us is God, who also has sealed us and given us the Spirit in our hearts as a deposit.

Believers have been anointed by God, and the Spirit of God's presence in our lives is the proof of this. We have been chosen by God and selected to do His will and purpose.

First John 2:20 says, "You have an anointing from the Holy One, and you know all things." Verse 27 adds, "The anointing which you have received from Him abides in you."

The anointing of the Spirit of God upon our lives is a reminder that we have been uniquely chosen by God to do a special work for Him. Since a person is anointed by having oil poured on his head (like the priests and kings of the Old Testament), the oil becomes a symbol of the Holy Spirit's presence and the approval of God.

7. *The symbol of a guarantee.*

In Ephesians 1:14 the Holy Spirit is called "the guarantee of our inheritance." The King James version uses the word "earnest." It refers to a down payment. Second Corinthians 1:22 says, "who also has sealed us and given us the Spirit in our hearts as a deposit." The word "deposit" is the same Greek word that is translated "guarantee" in Ephesians 1:14. Also, 2 Corinthians 5:5 says, "He who has prepared us for this very thing is God, who also has given us the Spirit as a guarantee."

Ephesians 1:13 states that those who believe in Jesus Christ are "sealed with the Holy Spirit of promise." The "seal" indicates ownership and security. It is the guarantee of future blessings. Modern Greek uses the word translated "deposit" or "guarantee" for an engagement ring. The presence of the Holy Spirit in our lives is God's engagement ring, a firm promise of the marriage and our inheritance in the future! What wonderful assurance to our hearts!

A Final Summary

The Holy Spirit is symbolized by the following:

Fire: symbolizing His power and purification.

Dove:	symbolizing His purity and peacefulness.
Wind:	symbolizing His power, sovereignty, and invisible work.
Water:	symbolizing the gift of eternal life.
Clothing:	symbolizing the power to witness.
Oil:	symbolizing God's approval and choice.
Guarantee:	symbolizing His ownership and our security.

These symbols describe the Spirit in terms of His attributes as well as His work in the believer's life.

To say that we are filled with the Spirit is to make some incredible claims. God is filling us with His own presence and power. A real Person has come to live in our bodies and seeks to control what we think, say, and do without annihilating our unique personalities or eliminating our right to choose and make decisions. He does not force us to be what God wants us to be. We are not robots. He draws us by His love and encourages us with His infinite resources, some of which He displays in our lives.

In the light of who the Holy Spirit is, it is very difficult to understand why a believer would not want to be controlled every moment of his life by the Holy Spirit of God. What wonderful possibilities await us who desire to be filled with the Spirit!

2

What Happened On The Day Of Pentecost?

Pentecost is a Jewish celebration which is conducted 50 days after the Sabbath of the week in which the feast of Passover is celebrated. Jews celebrate the following feasts during their religious year:

Passover:
: Fourteenth day of the first month (not January, but in the spring; Jews call it Nisan).

Unleavened Bread:
: Starts on the fifteenth day of Nisan and continues for seven days.

Firstfruits:
: Starts the day after the Sabbath of the week in which Passover is celebrated (on Sunday).

Weeks (or Pentecost):
: Starts 50 days after the Sabbath before Firstfruits (on Sunday).

Trumpets:
: First day of seventh month of Jewish religious year.

Atonement:	Tenth day of seventh month.
Tabernacles:	Starts the fifteenth day of seventh month and continues for seven more days—a total of eight days.

The information regarding these seven feasts is recorded in Leviticus 23. Many Jews also celebrate the feast of Purim, commemorating the events of the book of Esther, when God used her to spare the lives of Jewish people. Also, many Jews celebrate the feast of Hanukkah, or festival of lights, which commemorates the victory of the Jews over Antiochus Epiphanes, who had desecrated their temple. The New Testament refers to this feast and calls it the feast of "dedication" (John 10:22).

The biblical instruction regarding the feast of Weeks (Pentecost) is found in Leviticus 23:15-22:

> You shall count for yourselves from the day after the Sabbath, from the day that you brought the sheaf of the wave offering: seven Sabbaths shall be completed. Count fifty days to the day after the seventh Sabbath; then you shall offer a new grain offering to the Lord. You shall bring from your habitations two wave loaves of two-tenths of an ephah. They shall be of fine flour; they shall be baked with leaven. They are the firstfruits to the Lord. And you shall offer with the bread seven lambs of the first year, without blemish, one young bull, and two rams. They shall be as a burnt offering to the Lord, with their grain offering and their drink offerings, an offering made by fire for a sweet aroma to the Lord. Then you shall sacrifice one kid of the goats as a sin offering, and two male lambs of the first year as a sacrifice of peace

offering. The priest shall wave them with the bread of the firstfruits as a wave offering before the Lord, with the two lambs. They shall be holy to the Lord for the priest. And you shall proclaim on the same day that it is a holy convocation to you. You shall do no customary work on it. It shall be a statute forever in all your dwellings throughout your generations. When you reap the harvest of your land, you shall not wholly reap the corners of your field when you reap, nor shall you gather any gleaning from your harvest. You shall leave them for the poor and for the stranger: I am the Lord your God.

The Jewish name is "feast of Weeks." "Pentecost" is a Greek word meaning "fifty." This feast was one of three Jewish festivals that required every Jewish male over 20 years old to attend. Exodus 34:22,23 includes Pentecost as one of those three:

You shall observe the Feast of Weeks, of the firstfruits of wheat harvest, and the Feast of Ingathering at the year's end. Three times in the year all your men shall appear before the Lord, the Lord God of Israel.

This is a celebration of the firstfruits of the wheat harvest and comes seven weeks after the presentation of the firstfruits of the barley harvest at the Jewish festival called "Firstfruits."

After the destruction of the temple in 70 A.D., Jews began to connect the feast of Pentecost with the giving of the law at Mount Sinai. According to Rabbi Eleazar ben Pedath (270 A.D.), Pentecost is the day on which the Torah was given.

However, biblical teachings connect this feast with the wheat harvest.

Jewish teaching concerning the dating of Pentecost follows the reasoning that it comes 50 days after the fifteenth day of Nisan, the feast of Unleavened Bread, which was to be a "holy convocation" or special Sabbath. This would cause the day of Pentecost to fall on different days of the week each year. Christian teaching argues that the 50 days follows the normal Sabbath day of the week in which Passover and Unleavened Bread begins. This would place the feast on Sunday of each year. The feast of Firstfruits which celebrates the barley harvest occurs the day after the Sabbath of Passover week. The New Testament connects that feast with the resurrection of Jesus Christ, which occurred on Sunday, the first day of the week (1 Corinthians 15:20-23).

Some Bible teachers see this order of events at the time of Jesus' crucifixion and resurrection:

> Thursday (Nisan 14): Passover (Last Supper).
> Friday (Nisan 15): Unleavened Bread (a special Sabbath; the day Jesus was crucified).
> Saturday (Nisan 16): the normal Sabbath of each week.
> Sunday (Nisan 17): Firstfruits (day of Jesus' resurrection).
> Sunday (50 days after the Sabbath of Nisan 16): Day of Pentecost; coming of the Holy Spirit.

Jewish days are counted from sundown to sundown. The Last Supper that Jesus ate with His disciples would have been on Thursday evening, the beginning of the feast of Unleavened Bread, and His resurrection would have occurred sometime after sundown on Saturday, the beginning of the feast of Firstfruits.

Celebrating Pentecost

No one could reap or use the harvest for personal reasons until the sheaf of wheat was brought as a "wave offering" to the Lord at this feast. It was a time of great joy and celebration. In addition to many animal sacrifices, the main offering of the day was the presentation of two loaves of bread made from the new wheat and baked with leaven. None of the bread was placed on the altar because it was leavened, but it was eaten by the priests.

When the "wave offering" of barley was presented at the feast of Firstfruits, the Jewish people could begin using the new grain as food, but not until seven weeks later, at the feast of Pentecost, could the new grain be used for sacrificial offerings.

The feast was concluded by eating communal meals to which the poor, the stranger, and the Levite were invited.

The feast of Firstfruits represents the first of the harvest and a sample of more to come, and so the application to the resurrection. Jesus Christ arose from the dead on the feast of Firstfruits; the rest of the harvest of which He is the "firstfruits" began to be reaped on the day of Pentecost, when the Holy Spirit of God came and the church of Jesus Christ was born.

The day of Pentecost mentioned in Acts 2 is one of the great events of history. A mighty harvest began to be reaped and has continued now for over 1900 years! The reasons why the majority of Christians today worship on Sunday is twofold:

1. To celebrate the resurrection of Jesus Christ.
2. To celebrate the coming of the Holy Spirit

and the beginning of the church.

Both events occurred on Sunday.

The Holy Spirit Before Pentecost

As we mentioned in Chapter 1, the Holy Spirit was involved in the creation of the universe and of humanity. He was also involved in the writing of Scripture. We might call Him the Author of the Bible, though some 40 human writers were also involved. Consider the following:

1. *The Holy Spirit was controlling the writers of the Bible.*

   Second Peter 1:20,21 states:

   > Knowing this first, that no prophecy of Scripture is of any private interpretation, for prophecy never came by the will of man, but holy men of God spoke as they were moved by the Holy Spirit.

   The key word is *moved.* In Acts 27:14-17 Paul was involved in a storm, and the ship he was on lost control, so that the storm was directing their movements. Verse 17 says, "They struck sail and so were driven." The word "driven" is the same Greek word as "moved" in 2 Peter 1:21. Just as the storm was controlling the movements of that ship, so the Holy Spirit controlled the writers of Scripture so that what was written was not the product of their own ingenuity, but was guaranteed to be what God wanted said—accurate and totally reliable. That's what we mean by the inspiration of the Bible.

2. *The writers of Scripture declared that the Holy Spirit was speaking through them.*

King David's last words are recorded in 2 Samuel 23. In verse 2 we read, "The Spirit of the Lord spoke by me, and His word was on my tongue."

Ezekiel 2:2 records: "The Spirit entered me when He spoke to me, and set me on my feet; and I heard Him who spoke to me." This passage seems to indicate direct revelation from the Holy Spirit to the prophet. In verse 7 he is told, "You shall speak My words to them."

3. *Jesus said that the Holy Spirit was involved in the writing of Scripture.*

In Matthew 22:43 Jesus said, "How then does David in the Spirit call Him 'Lord,' saying," and then He quotes from Psalm 110:1. Jesus said that David uttered those words in Psalm 110 "in the Spirit."

4. *The apostle Peter said that the Holy Spirit was speaking through the Old Testament writers.*

In the upper room, where 120 disciples had gathered, a replacement for Judas among the 12 apostles was to be selected. Peter quoted the Scriptures regarding the events surrounding Judas, and made this statement in Acts 1:16:

> Men and brethren, this Scripture had to be fulfilled, which the Holy Spirit spoke by the mouth of David concerning Judas, who became a guide to those who arrested Jesus.

5. *The apostle Paul said that the Holy Spirit was speaking to and through the Old Testament writers.*

In Acts 28:25 Paul said, "The Holy Spirit spoke rightly through Isaiah the prophet to our fathers." Then he quoted from Isaiah 6.

In Hebrews 3:7 he began a quotation from Psalm 95: "Therefore, as the Holy Spirit says." In Hebrews 10:15-17 he quoted from Jeremiah 31 and prefaced it with this remark: "The Holy Spirit also witnesses to us; for after He had said before."

It is obvious from the above that the Holy Spirit was quite active in the days before Pentecost in terms of the writing of Scripture. He had already come to earth in that sense of working in the lives of human authors.

Another interesting work of the Holy Spirit before the day of Pentecost in Acts 2 is that of His control of evil. Genesis 6:3 comments on this ministry of the Spirit when it says concerning the wickedness of the generation who lived before the flood, "My Spirit shall not strive with man forever."

When the children of Israel were rebelling against God in the days of their wilderness wanderings, the Holy Spirit was at work among them. Nehemiah 9:20 says, "You also gave Your good Spirit to instruct them." Paul argues the same thing in Hebrews 3:7-19 and informs us that the Holy Spirit is speaking to us today by what He said in the past to His people concerning the hardening of our hearts and our unbelief.

Spirit-Filled People

Were people filled with the Spirit before Pentecost? An emphatic yes! Exodus 28:3 says of those who designed the high priest's garments, "I have filled [them] with the spirit of wisdom."

Consider Exodus 31:3, where it says of a craftsman named Bezaleel:

> I have filled him with the Spirit of God, in
> wisdom, in understanding, in knowledge, and
> in all manner of workmanship.

This commendation is repeated in Exodus 35:31.

There were individuals in the Old Testament who were filled with the Holy Spirit, not only for the writing of Scripture, but also for the designing and making of beautiful garments and furnishings for the tabernacle.

The Holy Spirit was also performing supernatural feats of strength through people. Judges 14:6 speaks of the ability of Samson to tear a lion apart, and says of him, "The Spirit of the Lord came mightily upon him."

This statement is repeated in Judges 14:19, when he kills 30 men, and in Judges 15:14,15, when he breaks the ropes and chains around him and kills 1000 men with the jawbone of a donkey!

The Holy Spirit also came upon people and caused them to prophesy. Numbers 11:25 speaks of 70 elders who prophesied because of the Holy Spirit's power, though they never did it again. Numbers 11:26-29 speaks of the Spirit's ministry in the lives of Eldad and Medad, two men who prophesied because of the Holy Spirit's presence and power. In Numbers 24:2 we learn that Balaam the prophet spoke because "the Spirit of God came upon him." Even king Saul prophesied through the help of the Holy Spirit to a group of prophets, according to 1 Samuel 10:10: "The Spirit of God came upon him, and he prophesied among them."

Prophesying involves public speaking, and of course people can do that without the Holy Spirit's help. But the prophesying mentioned in these Bible passages refers to speaking the word of God, and that takes the intervention of the Holy Spirit. Without the Holy Spirit's help, no one could speak by direct revelation from God.

It was said of Joshua, the leader who replaced Moses (Deuteronomy 34:9), that he was "full of the spirit of wisdom." Since that usually is connected with the filling of the Holy Spirit, we would have to conclude that Joshua was a man in Old Testament times who was filled with the Holy Spirit.

Men like Othniel (Judges 3:9,10) and Gideon (Judges 6:34), judges in ancient Israel, were described as men upon whom the Spirit of God came. Their leadership needed to be Spirit-filled, as ours does today.

Before the day of Pentecost it was said of John the Baptist, "He will also be filled with the Holy Spirit, even from his mother's womb" (Luke 1:15). We can see the work of the Holy Spirit in the life of a man named Simeon (Luke 2:25-35): "The Holy Spirit was upon him"; "it had been revealed to him by the Holy Spirit"; "he came by the Spirit into the temple." It was said of Jesus in Luke 4:1, ". . . being filled with the Holy Spirit," and that He "was led by the Spirit into the wilderness."

Before the day of Pentecost, in Acts 2, the Holy Spirit was actively involved in the lives of people. He came upon them for special ministries and times, and He also departed from certain individuals (cf. Judges 13:25 and 16:20 as well as 1 Samuel 10:10 and 16:14).

The Changed Ministry

A distinct change took place in the Holy Spirit's ministry after the day of Pentecost. Jesus Himself indicated what that difference was when He gave these words in John 14:16,17 to His disciples:

> I will pray the Father, and He will give you another Helper, that He may abide with you forever, even the Spirit of truth, whom the world cannot receive, because it neither sees Him nor knows Him; but you know Him, *for He dwells with you and will be in you.*

To His disciples before Pentecost in Acts 2 Christ said that the Holy Spirit "dwells *with* you." The Greek preposition translated "with" (*para*) means "alongside of." His next statement deals with the ministry of the

Spirit in their lives after the day of Pentecost: "and will be *in* you." Christians speak of the indwelling of the Holy Spirit and base it on this promise of Jesus. The Holy Spirit did not indwell believers in the Old Testament on a permanent basis, as He does today. In John 14:16 Jesus said that the Holy Spirit would be with us forever.

First Corinthians 6:19 speaks of this indwelling presence of the Holy Spirit in the lives of all believers when it says:

> Do you not know that your body is a temple of the Holy Spirit *who is in you*, whom you have from God, and you are not your own?

You must have the Holy Spirit dwelling in you today or you are not a Christian! Romans 8:9 makes this quite clear when it says:

> You are not in the flesh but in the Spirit, if indeed the Spirit of God dwells in you. Now if anyone does not have the Spirit of Christ, he is not His.

If you don't have the Holy Spirit indwelling you, you do not belong to Jesus Christ.

Jesus clearly indicated that a brand-new ministry of the Holy Spirit would begin on the day of Pentecost. In Luke 24:49 He said, "Behold, I send the Promise of My Father upon you; but tarry in the city of Jerusalem until you are endued with power from on high." The "Promise of the Father" refers to the work and ministry of the Holy Spirit from the day of Pentecost onward. This is clear from Acts 1:4,5:

> Being assembled together with them, He commanded them not to depart from

Jerusalem, but to wait for the Promise of the
Father, "which," He said, "you have heard
from Me; for John truly baptized with water,
but you shall be baptized with the Holy Spirit
not many days from now."

The "Promise of the Father" is the baptism of the Holy
Spirit, which the disciples had not yet experienced. It
would happen "not many days from now." How many
days would they have to wait? After His resurrection,
Christ was seen on earth for 40 days (Acts 1:3). Since
Pentecost comes 50 days after the Sabbath, the day
before Christ rose from the dead, that leaves just nine
or ten days that the disciples would have to wait until
this new ministry of the Spirit would begin.

Fulfilled Prophecy

The day of Pentecost in Acts 2 was a very important
event in God's prophetic program. Long ago (about
4000 years) God said to Abraham in Genesis 12:1-3:

Get out of your country, from your kindred
and from your father's house, to a land that
I will show you. I will make you a great nation;
I will bless you and make your name great;
and you shall be a blessing. I will bless those
who bless you, and I will curse him who
curses you; and in you all the families of the
earth shall be blessed.

In Genesis 15:5 God said to Abraham:

Look now toward heaven, and count the
stars if you are able to number them . . . . So
shall your descendants be.

Galatians 3:8,9 says:

> The Scripture, forseeing that God would justify the nations [Gentiles] by faith, preached the gospel to Abraham beforehand, saying, "In you all the nations shall be blessed." So then those who are of faith are blessed with believing Abraham.

These passages reveal that God would fulfill His promise to Abraham about His descendants by causing many Gentiles to believe. That's what happened on the day of Pentecost God began a new work of the Holy Spirit by which He is bringing many Gentiles to faith in the God of Abraham through a son of Abraham, the Messiah Himself, Jesus Christ our Lord!

The Outpoured Spirit

When the Holy Spirit came on the day of Pentecost, as recorded in Acts 2, Peter said this to the crowd who saw and heard some unusual manifestations of the Spirit's presence and power (Acts 2:14-21):

> Men of Judea and all who dwell in Jerusalem, let this be known to you, and heed my words. For these are not drunk, as you suppose, since it is only the third hour of the day. But this is what was spoken by the prophet Joel: "And it shall come to pass in the last days, says God, that I will pour out of My Spirit on all flesh; your sons and your daughters shall prophesy, your young men shall see visions, your old men shall dream dreams. And on My menservants and on My maidservants I will pour out My Spirit in those days; and they shall prophesy. I will show

wonders in heaven above and signs in the earth beneath: blood and fire and vapor of smoke. The sun shall be turned into darkness, and the moon into blood, before the coming of the great and notable day of the Lord. And it shall come to pass that whoever calls on the name of the Lord shall be saved."

Peter says that this was a fulfillment of prophecy. It was the promised outpouring of the Holy Spirit by which God would bring a multitude of Gentiles to Himself.

A confirmation that this is what happened on the day of Pentecost is found in Acts 10:44,45, when Peter introduced the gospel to the Gentiles through a Roman centurion named Cornelius:

While Peter was still speaking these words, the Holy Spirit fell upon all those who heard the word. And those of the circumcision [Jews] who believed were astonished, as many as came with Peter, because the gift of the Holy Spirit had been poured out on the Gentiles also.

The "last days" in which God is pouring out His Spirit to bring a multitude of Gentiles to Himself to fulfill His promise to Abraham actually began on the day of Pentecost and will continue until Christ comes again to this earth.

The outpouring of the Spirit will culminate in a great conversion of Israel. Zechariah 12:10 speaks of it:

I will pour on the house of David and on the inhabitants of Jerusalem the Spirit of grace and supplication; then they will look on Me whom they have pierced; they will mourn for Him as one mourns for his only son, and grieve for Him as one grieves for a first-born.

Ezekiel 39:27-29 confirms this when it says:

> "When I have brought them back from the peoples and gathered them out of their enemies' lands, and I am hallowed in them in the sight of many nations, then they shall know that I am the Lord their God, who sent them into captivity among the nations, but also brought them back to their own land, and left none of them captive any longer. And I will not hide My face from them anymore; for I shall have poured out My Spirit on the house of Israel," says the Lord God.

For Israel to be saved in that day and turn to their Messiah will require the same ministry that the Gentiles must experience—the outpouring of the Holy Spirit.

The Events of Pentecost

The Holy Spirit began His ministry of bringing a multitude of Gentiles to a saving knowledge of Jesus Christ. Both Jew and Gentile would now be bound together by the indwelling presence of the Holy Spirit and the baptism of the Spirit—placed into one body of people which we call the church of Jesus Christ. What a mystery!

The day of Pentecost started the following:

1. The outpouring of the Holy Spirit.
2. The permanent indwelling of the Holy Spirit.
3. The baptism of the Holy Spirit.
4. The church of Jesus Christ.

Some Bible interpreters believe that the significance of the two loaves of bread which were used as a "wave offering" at the Jewish feast of Weeks (Pentecost) is that they represent Jew and Gentile blended into one loaf beginning with the Holy Spirit's work mentioned in Acts 2.

Paul said in 1 Corinthians 10:17:

> We, being many, are one bread and one body; for we all partake of that one bread.

Ephesians 2:14-18 mentions this blending of Jew and Gentile together when it says:

> He Himself is our peace, who has made both one, and has broken down the middle wall of division between us, having abolished in His flesh the enmity, that is, the law of commandments contained in ordinances, so as to create in Himself one new man from the two, thus making peace, and that He might reconcile them both to God in one body through the cross, thereby putting to death the enmity. And He came and preached peace to you who were afar off and to those who were near. For through Him we both have access by one Spirit to the Father.

Jew and Gentile in one body—the church of Jesus Christ!

The coming of the Holy Spirit (outpouring) on the day of Pentecost is recorded in Acts 2. These 47 verses contain the following three things:

1. Unusual manifestations upon 120 believers (Acts 2:1-13).
2. A sermon by Peter (Acts 2:14-40).
3. A detailed description of the results,

explaining how the church began and functioned (Acts 2:41-47).

Unusual Manifestations

A great many Christians today are interested in repeating the unusual manifestations that occurred on the day of Pentecost as recorded in Acts 2. Whether that is possible will be discussed later. At this point it is important to realize that these manifestations were unusual. It was not normal in the lives of these people, either for the ones experiencing it or for the ones hearing about it. The coming of the Holy Spirit in fulfillment of Bible prophecies about the last days, when God would bring Gentiles to Himself through the pouring out of His Spirit, demands clear evidence. There should be undeniable proof that the Spirit actually came. There should be signs.

The basic facts of what initially happened to the 120 believers gathered in the upper room (Acts 1:12-15) are recorded in Acts 2:1-4:

> When the Day of Pentecost had fully come, they were all with one accord in one place. And suddenly there came a sound from heaven, as of a rushing mighty wind, and it filled the whole house where they were sitting. Then there appeared to them divided tongues, as of fire, and one sat upon each of them. And they were all filled with the Holy Spirit and began to speak with other tongues, as the Spirit gave them utterance.

Our discussion in this book centers on the question "Are you filled with the Holy Spirit?" Acts 2:4 says, "They were all filled with the Holy Spirit." It would seem that the filling of the Spirit should be characterized by what happened on that day unless the Bible gives further insight and instruction to the contrary.

The 120 Believers

At least the following occurred to the 120 believers:

1. *There was a sound from heaven.*
2. *There was an appearance of divided tongues upon each of them.*
3. *They were all filled with the Holy Spirit.*
4. *They began to speak with other tongues.*

There is no record in the New Testament that the sound or appearance of divided tongues ever occurred again, even though we read frequently about believers being filled with the Holy Spirit. We read of believers speaking in tongues in at least two other passages in Acts (10:46 and 19:6), and we have a rather lengthy discussion about tongues and other gifts in 1 Corinthians chapters 12-14.

Other believers (besides the 120) were filled with the Holy Spirit and other believers spoke in tongues, but there is no record that the sound or appearance of tongues happened again.

A Sound from Heaven

We learned earlier that the wind is a symbol of the Holy Spirit's presence and power (used by Jesus in John 3:8). In Acts 2:2 the sound from heaven is compared to "a rushing mighty wind." The Bible says that it "filled the whole house where they were sitting."

In January of each year we have some strong winds in our area. Our two-story house is so constructed that our master bedroom is located on the side where these winds blow. When they start pounding against our windows and house, we simply cannot sleep. The noise is tremendous. These winds (up to 85 miles an hour) can do great damage; they have torn up huge trees in our yard. As I consider those winds with their noise and power, I am reminded of what happened on the day of Pentecost.

Acts 2:6 reports that "when this sound occurred, the multitude came together." Evidently the sound attracted the crowd. The upper room on mount Zion is not far from the general temple area. The noise brought the crowds.

Tongues As of Fire

This was certainly an unusual manifestation of the Spirit's presence. But how appropriate! Beginning with this day of Pentecost, God was going to pour out His Spirit and bring a multitude of Gentiles to Himself. God was going to accomplish this by putting His Spirit's power into the lives of believers, who would then use their tongues to proclaim the message of salvation to the whole world. What a marvelous way to demonstrate what God was going to do! He gave them a visual aid— the appearance of divided tongues upon each of them. It was on each of them because God wanted *all* believers to witness through the power of the Spirit—not just the apostles.

This appearance of tongues seemed like tongues of fire. The passage does not say that they actually were fire, but only that they *appeared* "as of fire." They looked like tongue-shaped flames.

It is interesting to observe that the Bible does not say that these believers were praying at the time this unusual event occurred. It happened while they were "sitting" (Acts 2:2). This unusual manifestation was unrelated to their prayers or any past experiences. It happened in fulfillment of God's promise to pour out His Spirit in the last days. It came "when the day of Pentecost had fully come." The words "had fully come" are simply "was fulfilled." Luke, the author of Acts, is emphasizing the timing of God and the fulfillment of prophecy.

This unusual manifestation never occurred again. Its purpose was simply to announce the arrival of the Holy Spirit and the beginning of God's prophetic program for the last days.

Filled by the Spirit

The Bible is clear when it says, "They were *all* filled with the Holy Spirit." No one was left out. The next time we read of the believers experiencing the filling of the Holy Spirit is in Acts 4:31. It reads:

> When they had prayed, the place where they were assembled together was shaken; and they were all filled with the Holy Spirit, and they spoke the word of God with boldness.

There is no mention of a sound from heaven or of an appearance of tongues as of fire. There is no mention of anyone speaking with tongues, but rather of speaking with boldness. But once again, it *does* say that they were all filled with the Holy Spirit. We do not know how many people were involved in this assembly, but the filling of the Holy Spirit was for all of them, not just for the apostles or a few unusually gifted individuals. That's important for all of us to understand about the filling of the Holy Spirit.

What About Speaking in Tongues?

This issue is of such importance that we have devoted several chapters to it in this book. At this point we simply want to mention what it was that these 120 believers experienced.

The Bible says that they "began to speak with other tongues." What is meant by "other tongues"?

There are two Greek words translated by the English word "other." One word means "another of the same kind" and the other word means "another of a different kind." The latter word appears here in Acts 2:4. These tongues were different from their normal experience. But what is meant by the word "tongues"?

The Bible seems to clear this matter up when it says in Acts 2:6, "Everyone heard them speak in his own language." The word "language" is from the Greek word that gives us our English word "dialect." Acts 2:8 emphasizes this point even more when it says, "How is it that we hear, each in our own language [dialect] *in which we were born?*"

These tongues were *languages*, actual dialects spoken by the Jews gathered for the feast of Pentecost. These Jews came from many different parts and language groups of the Roman Empire (listing in Acts 2:9-11). Each of them was hearing these believers speak about the wonderful works of God in his own dialect. What a wonderful way for God to announce the outpouring of His Holy Spirit in the last days! The challenge is to reach the whole world—every language and dialect. The method is for believers to be filled with the Holy Spirit and to use their tongues to proclaim His message!

A Sermon by Peter

Peter referred to the prophecy of Joel concerning the outpouring of the Holy Spirit in the last days and indicated that these unusual manifestations were proof that the prophecy was now being filled. Peter spoke of the miracles of Jesus, His crucifixion and resurrection, His postresurrection appearances, and His present exalted position. He made use of Old Testament passages to prove his points.

The multitude listening to him were deeply convicted and cried out, "What shall we do?" Peter responded (Acts 2:38):

> Repent, and let every one of you be baptized in the name of Jesus Christ for the remission of sins; and you shall receive the gift of the Holy Spirit.

He then mentioned (v. 39) that the gift of the Holy Spirit is *the promise*, which was not only for the Jews ("to you and to your children") but also for the Gentiles ("to all who are afar off, as many as the Lord our God will call").

The Results Described

What exciting events these were! According to Acts 2:41, about three thousand people became believers that day. The church was born, a work of the Holy Spirit!

The addition of the 3000 believers to the 120 was done on the basis of two things:

1. Belief: "those who gladly received his word."
2. Baptism: "were baptized."

Baptism is the outward public testimony to the inward belief of the heart.

From Acts 2:42-47 we learn that the church that was begun by the work of the Holy Spirit was characterized by the following:

1. Continual dedication to apostolic teaching and fellowship, the breaking of bread, and prayers (v. 42).

2. Apostolic miracles (v. 43).
3. Unity and care for each other's needs (v. 44,45).
4. Frequent meetings and meals together (v. 46).
5. Praise toward God and favor with the people (v. 47a).
6. Constant evangelism (v. 47b).

What a tremendous thing the Holy Spirit did on that day of Pentecost, when believers were filled with the Holy Spirit!

Certain unusual manifestations were not repeated, but the work of God that was begun on that day continues until this very day. God is still filling believers with His Holy Spirit and using them to bring a multitude of people to faith in Jesus Christ and membership in the body of Christ, the church.

What a day that was!

3

Are You Baptized
With The Spirit?

Four great events occurred on the day of Pentecost, as recorded in Acts 2:

1. The outpouring of the Holy Spirit.
2. The permanent indwelling of the Holy Spirit.
3. The beginning of the church.
4. The baptism of the Holy Spirit.

The baptism of the Holy Spirit is greatly misunderstood by many believers. It is made to be something which the Bible does not teach, and it is often confused with the filling of the Holy Spirit. To many believers these two questions are the same:

1. Are you filled with the Spirit?
2. Are you baptized with the Spirit?

But they are not the same! The purposes of each are very different.

The Timing of the Baptism

No one was baptized by the Holy Spirit before the day of Pentecost. The Holy Spirit was certainly active in the days of the Old Testament; He filled various individuals and His power was upon believers (then as now). However, there is not one verse in the Bible to prove that His baptism ministry ever occurred before the day of Pentecost.

According to Acts 1:4,5 the baptism of the Spirit had not occurred at that point:

> Being assembled together with them, He commanded them not to depart from Jerusalem, but to wait for the Promise of the Father, "which," He said, "you have heard from Me; for John truly baptized with water, but you shall be baptized with the Holy Spirit not many days from now."

The baptism of the Holy Spirit was to take place "not many days from now." These words of Jesus ought to settle any questions we may have as to when the baptism originally took place. Again, this is not speaking of the *filling* of the Spirit, which had occurred in previous history.

What Is the Baptism?

The baptism of the Spirit is mentioned seven times in the New Testament. In each case the preposition in Greek is the same. It is translated either "by" the Spirit or "with" the Spirit or "in" the Spirit, but all seven passages contain exactly the same Greek preposition. Consider these passages carefully. Six of the seven passages compare the baptism of the Holy Spirit with the water baptism of John the Baptist.

Matthew 3:11—I indeed baptize you with water unto repentance, but He who is coming after me is mightier than I, whose sandals I am not worthy to carry. He will baptize you with the Holy Spirit and fire.

Mark 1:8—I indeed baptized you with water, but He will baptize you with the Holy Spirit.

Luke 3:16—John answered, saying to them all, "I indeed baptize you with water; but One mightier than I is coming, whose sandal strap I am not worthy to loose. He will baptize you with the Holy Spirit and with fire."

John 1:33—I did not know Him, but He who sent me to baptize with water said to me, "Upon whom you see the Spirit descending, and remaining on Him, this is He who baptizes with the Holy Spirit."

Acts 1:5—John truly baptized with water, but you shall be baptized with the Holy Spirit not many days from now.

Acts 11:16 Then I remembered the word of the Lord, how He said, "John indeed baptized with water, but you shall be baptized with the Holy Spirit."

The seventh passage is the specific one which gives us some insight as to what the baptism of the Holy Spirit is intended to accomplish. First Corinthians 12:13 says:

By one Spirit we were all baptized into one body—whether Jews or Greeks, whether slaves or free—and have all been made to drink into one Spirit.

According to this verse, the baptism of the Holy Spirit is that work of the Spirit which makes us all one body in Jesus Christ. In other words, the baptism of the

Spirit forms the church, the body of Christ.

The gentleman in my office was quite cordial, though somewhat aggressive. He said that the Lord had spoken to him and instructed him to help me understand the baptism of the Holy Spirit, which he said I was teaching incorrectly. He proceeded to give me his view. He was especially disturbed over my teaching that the baptism of the Holy Spirit forms the body of Christ and that this action by the Spirit is the intention of God behind the baptism of the Spirit.

I asked this gentleman to give me Scripture to support his views about the baptism of the Spirit. What followed was a great disappointment. He kept twisting the statements of Scripture and adding his own viewpoints. When I questioned him on this, he said that his experiences proved that his view was the correct one. When I showed him 1 Corinthians 12:13 and asked him what he thought it meant, he told me that there were two baptisms. He said the one in 1 Corinthians 12:13 is the baptism "by the Spirit," which does form the body of Christ, but the baptism "with the Spirit," was something quite different. When I pointed out that the preposition was exactly the same in Greek in both cases, he began to criticize me for being too academic! I finally decided that it was impossible to win with this gentleman's methods of argument.

It saddens many Bible teachers to hear of the confusion which many believers have over the baptism of the Holy Spirit—a marvelous work which God began on the day of Pentecost, a work by which He forms the church, a work through which He is calling out a great multitude of believers from every tribe, tongue, and nation to fulfill His promise of long ago to Abraham (Genesis 12:3).

Why the Confusion?

The primary problem deals with the unusual

manifestations recorded in the book of Acts which accompanied the baptism of the Holy Spirit. The manifestations are often confused with the baptism itself, and the original purpose of God for the baptism of the Spirit is ignored and something else substituted in its place.

If we understand the words of Jesus in Acts 1:4,5, the baptism of the Spirit did indeed take place on the day of Pentecost, though Acts 2 does not specifically state that it did. What it *does* say in Acts 2:4 is, "They were all filled with the Holy Spirit." It is not difficult to see why the filling of the Spirit is often confused with the baptism of the Spirit: They happened simultaneously on the day of Pentecost.

The manifestation (in addition to the sound of a powerful wind and the appearance of tongues of fire) which demonstrated that the baptism of the Spirit had taken place was the fact that these 120 believers "began to speak with other tongues, as the Spirit gave them utterance." At least on the day of Pentecost, the evidence of the baptism of the Holy Spirit was speaking in tongues. There is no denying that fact.

In Acts 10:44-48 we have the results of Peter's visit to the household of Cornelius, to whom he brought the gospel of Jesus Christ. It was the opening of the door to the Gentile world. The Jewish believers who were with Peter were astonished at the results, because once again the believers (in this case Gentile believers) spoke with tongues (v. 46).

In Acts 11:15-18 Peter is reviewing the events at the house of Cornelius to the apostles and brethren in Judea, who had heard that the Gentiles had also received the Word of God. He said in verse 15:

> As I began to speak, the Holy Spirit fell upon them, as upon us at the beginning.

Peter clearly identifies this experience as being the same as the one in Acts 2 on the day of Pentecost. He also mentions in verse 16 that their experience involved the baptism of the Holy Spirit.

There is only one more instance where the book of Acts specifically mentions people who spoke in tongues—Acts 19. We read in verse 6:

> When Paul had laid hands on them, the
> Holy Spirit came upon them, and they spoke
> with tongues and prophesied.

Although it does not mention that they were baptized with the Spirit, the text seems to indicate that this probably took place. Paul's question in Acts 19:2 to these 12 men who claimed to be disciples (probably disciples of John the Baptist through the ministry of Apollos— cf. Acts 18:24-28 with 19:1-4) was:

> Did you receive the Holy Spirit when you
> believed?

When they replied that they knew nothing about the Holy Spirit, he asked them (Acts 19:3):

> Into what then were you baptized?

They clearly responded that they were baptized after the teaching of John the Baptist. Since six of the seven passages which refer to the baptism with the Spirit compare it to John's baptism, it would seem logical to assume that this is the point in this passage. Therefore the statement in Acts 19:6, "the Holy Spirit came upon them," would refer to the baptism of the Holy Spirit.

In Acts 2, 10, and 19 it appears that the evidence for the baptism of the Holy Spirit was speaking in tongues. Does this mean that everyone who speaks in tongues is baptized with the Spirit? Or does this mean that you must speak with tongues in order to be baptized with the Spirit? Or does this mean that if you have never spoken in tongues, you are not baptized with the Spirit? Because of the importance of these questions (and others relating to the issue of speaking in tongues), we have reserved later chapters to deal with this issue.

It is also possible that the baptism of the Holy Spirit is being referred to in Acts 8:14-17:

> When the apostles who were at Jerusalem heard that Samaria had received the word of God, they sent Peter and John to them, who, when they had come down, prayed for them that they might receive the Holy Spirit. For as yet He had fallen upon none of them. They had only been baptized in the name of the Lord Jesus. Then they laid hands on them, and they received the Holy Spirit.

Is this also referring to the baptism with the Spirit? It is quite possible. The words here are "receive the Holy Spirit" and "fallen upon." In Acts 11:15 Peter says of the Gentile converts mentioned in Acts 10:44-48 that "the Holy Spirit fell upon them, as upon us at the beginning." Since this is a reference to the baptism of the Holy Spirit (as is clear from verse 16), we could conclude that the reference in Acts 8 which deals with Samaritan believers is also referring to the baptism of the Holy Spirit.

While there is no mention of tongues-speaking in Acts 8, it is not possible to rule this out. There was a visible proof of the Holy Spirit being received because Simon the sorcerer "saw" something. Acts 8:17,18 says:

> Then they laid hands on them, and they received the Holy Spirit. Now when Simon saw

that through the laying on of the apostles'
hands the Holy Spirit was given, he offered
them money.

What did Simon see? It is possible, even logical, to
believe that he saw proof by these Samaritan believers
speaking in tongues, just as Jewish believers did in Acts
2, Gentile believers did in Acts 10, and disciples of John
the Baptist did in Acts 19.

If our theory is correct, then the evidence of the
baptism of the Holy Spirit in the book of Acts is speaking
with tongues. It happened in four different locations:

Jerusalem—Acts 2 (Jewish believers)
Samaria—Acts 8 (Samaritan believers)
Caesarea—Acts 10 (Gentile believers)
Ephesus—Acts 19 (disciples of John the Baptist)

Another interesting fact deals with the laying on of
the apostles' hands. There is no mention of this in Acts
2 or 10, but it is emphasized in Acts 8 and 19. Apostolic
presence was evident in each case, however.

Acts 2—the 12 apostles (2:14)
Acts 8—Peter and John (8:14)
Acts 10—Peter (10:44)
Acts 19—Paul (19:6)

The presence and authority of the apostles seem
to be related to the issue of the unusual manifestations that took place in the beginning stages of the
Spirit's work in the book of Acts. Jesus said in Mark
16:17:

These signs will follow those who believe:
In My name they will cast out demons; they
will speak with new tongues.

Mark 16:20 states:

> They [the apostles] went out and preached everywhere, the Lord working with them and confirming the word through the accompanying signs.

Hebrews 2:3,4 concurs with this fact:

> How shall we escape if we neglect so great a salvation, which at the first began to be spoken by the Lord, and was confirmed to us by those [apostles] who heard Him, God also bearing witness both with signs and wonders, with various miracles, and gifts of the Holy Spirit, according to His own will?

Putting this all together, it appears that the apostles and their message needed to be confirmed or authenticated. God did this by unusual manifestations, which included speaking in tongues. The message about the outpouring of the Holy Spirit in the last days which Peter began to preach on the day of Pentecost was confirmed in the minds and hearts of those who heard the apostles teach about the church (the body of Christ) through the manifestation of speaking in tongues, as well as through other miracles.

The baptism of the Holy Spirit, by which Jews and Gentiles are placed into one body in Christ (the church), began on the day of Pentecost in Jerusalem among Jewish believers. It spread to Samaria, Caesarea, and Ephesus as God continued to give dramatic proof that the new age of the Spirit (a fulfillment of prophecy) had begun and that the whole world would be affected.

Are All Believers Spirit-Baptized?

On the basis of 1 Corinthians 12:13, *YES!*

The church in Corinth was described by Paul in 1 Corinthians 3:1-4 as "carnal." They were not a group of Spirit-filled believers—quite the contrary. Yet all of them had been baptized with the Holy Spirit.

. This does not mean, however, that they were Spirit-filled. It only means that the Holy Spirit had come to dwell within them because of their faith in Jesus Christ. They were born of the Spirit and He was now dwelling inside them. Paul made this point clear in 1 Corinthians 6:19:

> Do you not know that your body is the temple of the Holy Spirit who is in you, whom you have from God, and you are not your own?

This is extremely important to our understanding of the Spirit-filled life. You may have the Holy Spirit, but this doesn't mean that the Holy Spirit has you! If you are a believer in Jesus Christ as your Lord and Savior, you have been baptized with the Spirit; He indwells you. If He doesn't, you are not a believer. Romans 8:9 confirms this point when it says:

> You are not in the flesh but in the Spirit, if indeed the Spirit of God dwells in you. Now if anyone does not have the Spirit of Christ, he is not his.

If you do not have the Spirit, you don't belong to Christ!

But this doesn't guarantee that you are filled with the Holy Spirit. That is quite another matter.

How to Receive the Holy Spirit

Since it is crucial to our salvation, it is imperative that we understand and experience the coming of the Holy

Spirit into our own lives. Since the day of Pentecost, described in Acts 2, all believers are baptized, indwelt, and sealed with the presence of the Holy Spirit. Our bodies are temples of the Spirit; He dwells in them, and through them He manifests Himself to the world.

Christians have proposed many different ideas relating to how the Holy Spirit is received. Some suggest fervent prayer, or complete yieldedness, or obedience, or faith, etc. What does the Bible teach? The following passages relate to how a person receives the Holy Spirit: ✓

1. *By asking for it.* ? Jn 14: 13,14 ? 9/26/91

If you then, being evil, know how to give good gifts to your children, how much more will your heavenly Father give the Holy Spirit *to those who ask Him!* (Luke 11:13)

2. *By believing in the Lord Jesus Christ.*

This He spoke concerning the Spirit, whom *those believing in Him* would receive; for the Holy Spirit was not yet given, because Jesus was not yet glorified (John 7:39).

If therefore God gave them the same gift as He gave us *when we believed on the Lord Jesus Christ*, who was I that I could withstand God? (Acts 11:17).   ? Act 2 or Jn 20?

John indeed baptized with a baptism of repentance, saying to the people that *they should believe on Him who would come after him, that is, on Christ Jesus* (Acts 19:4).

3. *By obeying God.*

We are His witnesses to these things, and so also is the Holy Spirit whom God has given *to those who obey Him* (Acts 5:32). ? Jn 14:15 9/26/91
 ? 2 th 1:8

4. *By repenting and being baptized.*

Repent, and let every one of you *be baptized* in the name of Jesus Christ for the remission of sins; *and you shall receive the gift of the Holy Spirit* (Acts 2:38).

5. *Through the laying on of the apostles' hands.*

Then they *laid hands on them*, and they received the Holy Spirit (Acts 8:17).

When Paul had *laid hands on them*, the Holy Spirit came upon them, and they spoke with tongues and prophesied (Acts 19:6).

6. *By having Christ breathe on you.*

When He had said this, *He breathed on them*, and said to them, "Receive the Holy Spirit" (John 20:22).

7. *By waiting for it.*

Behold, I send the Promise of My Father upon you; but *tarry* (wait) in the city of Jerusalem until you are endued with power from on high (Luke 24:49).

Being assembled together with them, He commanded them not to depart from Jerusalem, but *to wait* for the Promise of the Father (Acts 1:4).

Are we to do all of these things in order to receive the baptism of the Holy Spirit?

First of all, those who were told to wait did absolutely nothing to receive the Spirit. He came on the day of Pentecost in fulfillment of Bible prophecy. Believers after Pentecost are never told to wait or tarry. Number 7 above is not a prerequisite for receiving the Spirit.

Second, those upon whom the apostles' hands were laid needed apostolic intervention and confirmation (Samaritans in Acts 8 and disciples of John the Baptist in Acts 19) that the new age of the Spirit had truly begun.

This is not needed today, nor are those apostles available! We have the Bible to read, and we can clearly see that the outpouring of the Holy Spirit has already begun.

Third, those upon whom Jesus breathed were the apostles, and obviously because Jesus is not physically here on earth today, such situations are no longer possible. It could be said, however, that every person who receives the Spirit today has been breathed on by Jesus Christ, at least in the sense that He is the One who baptizes us with the Spirit.

Fourth, the other conditions (asking, believing, obeying, and repenting) are all speaking of the same thing—faith in Jesus Christ as Lord and Savior.

Jesus said in John 14:17 that "the world cannot receive" the Holy Spirit. No unbeliever receives Him. The contrary is also true: Only believers receive Him!

Everyone who comes to Jesus Christ and believes on Him will receive the Holy Spirit, regardless of what feelings exist in that person's life at the time or what experiences may accompany that expression of faith. John 7:37-39 is the best passage on this matter. Jesus used the feast of Tabernacles to teach about how to receive the Spirit. The feast commemorated the Jewish wilderness wanderings. The occasion of Jesus' remarks was a celebration of how God brought water from a rock. The priests would pour out water from the golden vessels of the temple in honor of that miracle of God long ago. The passage says:

> On the last day, that great day of the feast, Jesus stood and cried out, saying, "If anyone thirsts, let him come to Me and drink. He who believes in Me, as the Scripture has said, out of his heart will flow rivers of living water." But this He spoke concerning the Spirit, whom those believing in Him would receive;

for the Holy Spirit was not yet given, because
Jesus was not yet glorified.

Jesus compares the drinking of water to believing in
Him. We should emphasize the phrase "if anyone
thirsts." We must recognize our need of the water of
the Spirit or else we probably will not drink.

When people receive the Spirit, they receive Him from
Jesus Christ. We must come to *Jesus Christ*, not to a
church or a way of doing things. The one prerequisite
for receiving the Spirit or being baptized by the Spirit
is, to believe on the Lord Jesus Christ.

Reception and Baptism

Is receiving the Spirit the same as being baptized by
the Spirit? In Acts 2:38,39 Peter said:

Repent, and let every one of you be
baptized in the name of Jesus Christ for the
remission of sins; and you shall receive the
gift of the Holy Spirit. For the promise is to
you and to your children, and to all who are
afar off, as many as the Lord our God will call.

The "gift of the Holy Spirit" is referred to as "the
promise." In Acts 1:4,5 Jesus told the disciples to wait
in Jerusalem for "the Promise of the Father," and in verse
5 He referred to it as the baptism of the Holy Spirit.

In Acts 11:15-18 the baptism of the Spirit is called
"the same gift" as Peter and the apostles had received
on the day of Pentecost, and Peters says that it came
"when we believed on the Lord Jesus Christ."

These terms appear to be equal:

BAPTISM = GIFT = PROMISE

Therefore, receiving the Holy Spirit is the same as
being baptized by the Holy Spirit.

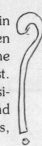

The only exception to this might be the incident in John 20:22, where the apostles received the Spirit when Jesus breathed on them. Yet they were baptized by the Holy Spirit a few days later, on the day of Pentecost. Naturally, an exception would occur during the transition from the ministry of Jesus with His disciples and the ministry of the Holy Spirit through the disciples, which began officially on the day of Pentecost.

Conviction by the Spirit

Some people believe that you cannot receive the Holy Spirit unless the Spirit convicts you and draws you to Christ. To carry it a step further, many Christians believe that you cannot believe on the Lord Jesus Christ unless you are born again by the Holy Spirit. The order would be something like this:

1. Conviction by the Spirit.
2. Regeneration by the Spirit (being born again).
3. Confession and repentance.
4. Faith in Jesus Christ.
5. Baptism, indwelling, and sealing of the Spirit.

It is difficult to separate these matters in an individual's response to the proclamation of the gospel. It seems on a human level that they operate together and often seem simultaneous.

In John 16:7-11 Jesus taught us concerning the convicting work of the Holy Spirit:

> I tell you the truth. It is to your advantage that I go away; for if I do not go away, the Helper will not come to you; but if I depart, I will send Him to you. And when He has

come, He will convict the world of sin, and
of righteousness, and of judgment: of sin,
because they do not believe in Me; of righteousness, because I go to My Father and you
see Me no more; of judgment, because the
ruler of this world is judged.

Notice that the Holy Spirit will "come to you,"
meaning to *believers*. The text says, "When He has
come, He will convict the world." The assumption is that
when He comes to the believers, He will convict unbelievers. It appears that the conviction of unbelievers by
the Holy Spirit is done through the lives of believers in
whom the Holy Spirit dwells.

The passage tells us that the Holy Spirit will convict
the world or unbelievers of three things: sin, righteousness, and judgment. A reason is given for each.

1. *Concerning sin* (John 16:9)

The reason for this conviction is "because they do not
believe in Me." Unbelievers are convicted because they
don't believe in Christ. If they did, they would feel no
conviction because they would be forgiven. The word
"sin" is singular, not plural. The sin involved is unbelief
or rejection of Jesus Christ. Believers, by exhibiting faith
in Jesus Christ and knowing confidently that their sins
are forgiven because of it, are used by the Holy Spirit
to convict those who don't.

In one sense, the conviction of the Holy Spirit about
sin could be likened to the person who thirsts. He knows
his need of water. Since Jesus Christ is the only One
who can take care of our sin, we will come to Him when
we are convicted of our sin by the Holy Spirit. The Spirit
draws us to Christ by convicting us of our sin.

2. *Concerning righteousness* (John 16:10)

The reason for this conviction is "because I go to My

Father and you see Me no more." The standard of righteousness and godliness was the life of Jesus Christ. While He was here, His life confronted unbelievers with their need. They simply did not measure up. Now that He is gone back to heaven, the Holy Spirit accomplishes the same thing in the lives of believers. We become the "salt of the earth" (Matthew 5:13) and the "light of the world" (Matthew 5:14-16) which unbelievers now see and by which they are drawn by the Holy Spirit to Jesus Christ.

3. *Concerning judgment* (John 16:11)

The reason for this conviction is "because the ruler of this world is judged." The "ruler of this world" is Satan. He could not defeat Christ at the cross. Through the resurrection, Christ won the victory and Satan was judged. The Holy Spirit raised Christ from the dead, according to Romans 8:11. The world is judged by the fact of the Spirit's presence in believers, proving that Christ rose from the dead and Satan was defeated. Through the presence and power of the Spirit in believers' lives, the unbeliever in convicted (becomes convinced) that Christianity is true. Jesus really did arise from the dead, and the enemy has been conquered!

It is obvious that the Holy Spirit convicts the world of unbelievers. It appears that He does so through His work in believers. It would be hard to conceive of a person coming to Jesus Christ and believing in Him without experiencing the convicting work of the Holy Spirit.

Jesus made it clear in John 6:44 that "no one can come to Me unless the Father who sent Me draws him." In John 6:63 He said, "It is the Spirit who gives life; the flesh profits nothing. The words that I speak to you are spirit, and they are life." Verse 64 says, "But there are some of you who do not believe." In verse 65 He repeated His earlier words from verse 44: "Therefore

I have said to you that no one can come to Me unless it has been granted to him by My Father."

On the basis of these verses it would appear that the Holy Spirit is the means which the Father uses to draw people to Jesus Christ, and that He does this drawing through the words which Jesus spoke. As the gospel is proclaimed, the Spirit convicts and draws people to Jesus Christ. Since no one can come to Christ without being drawn by the Father, it seems that the Spirit's conviction is necessary before a person can receive the Spirit.

Born Again by the Spirit

The Bible clearly teaches that we must be born again. The Spirit of God causes that to happen; we don't do it ourselves. Jesus said in John 3:3:

> Most assuredly I say to you, unless one is born again, he cannot see the kingdom of God.

In John 3:5 He said:

> Most assuredly I say to you, unless one is born of water and the Spirit, he cannot enter the kingdom of God.

John 3:7 says:

> You must be born again.

Just as we are born physically ("that which is born of the flesh is flesh"—John 3:6), so we are born spiritually ("that which is born of the Spirit is spirit") by the work of the Holy Spirit of God.

John 1:13 clarifies the fact that spiritual birth is not referring to physical descent, human desire, or human performance. It is based on the work of God alone. Titus 3:5 states:

> Not by works of righteousness which we have done, but according to His mercy He saved us, through the washing of regeneration and renewing of the Holy Spirit.

[handwritten note: Saved = Born Again? 9/21/91]

Clearly it is the Holy Spirit who does the regenerating. But 1 Peter 1:23-25 tells us that He uses the Word of God to do it:

> Having been born again, not of corruptible seed but incorruptible, through the word of God which lives and abides forever, because "All flesh is as grass, and all the glory of man as the flower of the grass. The grass withers, and its flower falls away, but the word of the Lord endures forever." Now this is the word which by the gospel was preached to you.

The Holy Spirit uses the incorruptible seed of the gospel to cause spiritual birth.

The Bible speaks of our responsibility to ask, believe, repent, or receive, but it also speaks of the Spirit's work of convicting, regenerating, baptizing, sealing, and indwelling. Our ability to receive the Spirit is based upon the work of the Spirit that convicts and draws us to Jesus Christ. The Spirit opens our eyes to the truth of the gospel and causes us to respond to its glorious message. The expected response from us is faith in what God says, leading us to confess that we are sinners, causing us to repent from our sinful ways, and drawing us to our only hope and Savior from sin, Jesus Christ our Lord.

If you have believed in the Lord Jesus Christ as your Savior, then you have received the Spirit and have been baptized by the Holy Spirit into the family of God.

4

What About
Spiritual Gifts?

After finishing a lecture on spiritual gifts to a group of graduate school students, one of the students asked, "Have you ever spoken in tongues?" I replied, "No." He then said, "Then you have no right to teach us about the gifts of the Spirit." In his view, a Spirit-filled believer is one who has spoken in tongues. The gift of tongues was crucial to his understanding about the whole subject of spiritual gifts.

That is often the case. After a series of radio messages on spiritual gifts, a man called me and inquired about whether I had spoken in tongues. When I told him I had not, he then accused me of not being Spirit-filled and incapable of teaching about spiritual gifts.

Before we deal with the crucial issue of speaking in tongues, we need to talk for a moment about the whole subject of spiritual gifts. When a person is Spirit-filled, the gifts of the Spirit will be used properly.

What Are Spiritual Gifts?

Spiritual gifts are abilities given to all believers that

allow them to minister effectively to other people. They are not merely natural talents or acquired skills; they are the result of the Holy Spirit's work in our lives. Every believer has at least one gift, according to 1 Peter 4:10, and we are expected to use it for the glory of God (verse 11).

An elderly lady who heard me speak on the subject of spiritual gifts remarked to me after the service, "I don't think the Lord gave me any gifts." I started to answer her, but before I could, a lady friend of hers spoke up and said, "Why, that's not true, Hazel. I don't know anyone who has the gift of showing mercy like you do. Your love and compassion for the sick is a gift for which many of us are deeply thankful." It reminded me of an important point: Other people know you in terms of your gifts better than you think. Every believer has at least one gift. It seems to me that some believers have more than one gift.

How Many Gifts Are There?

Christians disagree. Some say that the lists mentioned in the Bible are not complete, but are only a sampling. Others insist that the only spiritual gifts that exist are those that are specifically mentioned in the Bible. Among those who believe that the Bible contains a complete list of spiritual gifts, some say that certain gifts are no longer needed for today, now that we have a completed Bible. Others believe that all the gifts listed are still in operation today.

Spiritual Gifts in the Old Testament?

Certain men appear to have been gifted by God, but there is no specific teaching regarding spiritual gifts in the Old Testament, nor had the Holy Spirit's work of forming the body of Christ (the church) begun. Those who believe that there are gifts in the Old Testament usually point to the following:

1. *The gift of craftsmanship* (Exodus 28:3; 31:1-6; 36:1,2)

Two men, Bezaleel and Aholiab, are mentioned as men skilled to work on the tabernacle, especially in the area of carpentry and the cutting and designing of precious metals. The text of Exodus 31:3 says that Bezaleel was filled with the Spirit of God to do this work. Exodus 28:3 speaks of skillful or gifted persons to make the garments of the high priest.

2. *The gift of music* (1 Samuel 16:14-23)

David is called a skillful musician, and the Bible says that the Lord was with him. Some believe that this indicates a spiritual gift, though the Bible does not say so. David's skill worked wonders on the heart of Saul, causing an evil spirit to depart from him.

Those who believe in the spiritual gift of music often point to 1 Corinthians 14:26, which mentions those who have a "psalm." Psalming refers to a person who strikes a stringed instrument. Because the verse is dealing with other spiritual gifts, the assumption is that this is a reference to the spiritual gift of music. However, it could just be referring to the use of music and musical instruments in the meetings of the church. Psalming or striking a musical instrument is also mentioned in Ephesians 5:19 and Colossians 3:16.

John is a gifted musician, and most believers really enjoy his ministry of music. The interesting thing about him is that he is not well-trained in the music field. He sings with great compassion and tenderness. When you hear him, you feel that he knows your trials and struggles. When he is not singing, he often visits people who are sick. When he hears about someone who is in the hospital, he is quick to visit that person and try to help in whatever way he can. He manifests a great deal of joy when he calls on people, and many have spoken of the blessing he has been to them at times of physical difficulties. It seems to me that John exercises the spiritual gift of showing mercy through his music.

Most of us have met people who seem to have special abilities that others don't have. It isn't simply a matter of education or training. Two musicians with the same skill are often very much different in terms of the ability to minister to the hearts of believers. What explains the difference? It could be related to spiritual maturity or the experiences of those individuals. Some have the ability to communicate and empathize with an audience because of what they have experienced in their lives.

Unless the Old Testament clearly teaches the presence of spiritual gifts, it would seem wise not to argue too strongly about the so-called gifts of Old Testament times. We shouldn't rule them out, but without further evidence it is difficult to be dogmatic.

My musical background causes me to say an additional word about the possibility of a spiritual gift of music. I have observed over the years a great many musicians. Some very skilled people have no relationship to Jesus Christ at all. I have also seen some highly skilled Christians who did not seem to minister to the hearts of people. I have come to the conclusion that music is not a spiritual gift per se but that it is a gift from God (as all things are!). What I think happens when a person performs musically is that the spiritual gift which the person does have is usually communicated through the music. A person with a spiritual gift of exhortation (counseling) usually performs that way. A person with the gift of showing mercy often manifests it through the kinds of music performed as well as the manner in which it is done.

Gifted People Versus Gifts Given to People

According to Ephesians 4:11, there are four gifted people who are given to the church to help believers work together and minister their gifts to one another:

Apostles
Prophets
Evangelists
Pastor/teachers

Jesus Christ gives these gifted people to the church. The Holy Spirit also gives them spiritual gifts. These gifted people are responsible for equipping believers for spiritual ministry. This is primarily done through the preaching and teaching of the Bible (see 2 Timothy 3:16,17).

These gifted people are responsible to start churches by winning people to Jesus Christ, discipling them, and encouraging them to use their spiritual gifts to minister to others. Some of them will travel frequently and use their ministry in different cultures and cities. Others will stay in one local church, using their ministry to train and teach the believers in that church. Their primary task is to train and teach others, seeking ways to encourage and motivate them to use their spiritual gifts for the glory of God.

Gifts Mentioned in the New Testament

Romans 12:3-8 gives us a list of seven gifts, only one of which is mentioned elsewhere (prophecy). This particular listing emphasizes how the gifts are to be used.

Prophecy—according to the proportion of faith.
Ministry—in his ministering.

Teaching—in his teaching.
Exhorting—in his exhortation.
Giving—with liberality.
Leading—with diligence.
Showing mercy—with cheerfulness.

First Corinthians 12:8-10 lists nine gifts (including prophecy, which is mentioned in the Romans 12 list):

Word of wisdom
Word of knowledge

Faith
Gifts of healings
Working of miracles
Prophecy
Discerning of spirits

Kinds of tongues
Interpretation of tongues

The grammatical construction of this passage demands that there are three categories of gifts. We are not sure what the meaning of these categories is, but it is interesting to observe that a gift from each category is mentioned in 1 Corinthians 13:8, a text which shows the temporary nature of spiritual gifts when compared to God's love, which lasts forever.

First Corinthians 12:28 gives another listing of gifts, repeating some but adding two new ones—helps and administrations.

It is possible that two more gifts are listed in 1 Corinthians 7:7:

I wish that all men were even as I myself.
But each one has his own gift from God, one
in this manner and another in that.

What is Paul talking about when he mentions a "gift from God"? It appears that the two gifts are:

Singleness (or celibacy)
Marriage

Paul's word for "gift" is the Greek word from which we get our English word "charismatic." How do we explain the ability of some people to remain single without experiencing sexual pressure in their lives? Is this a gift of singleness? Paul seems to indicate that this is the case. If this is true, then there is also a gift of marriage—a person designed by God to be married.

While these two gifts are not normally put into the category of spiritual gifts, the apostle Paul seems to indicate that they are, especially the matter of remaining single in order to have a greater ministry for Christ.

Evelyn enjoyed being single and had a great desire to serve the Lord. Her problem was that her Christian friends kept encouraging her to get married. She had no desire or need to do so, but wondered if the Bible instructed her to get married. If it did, she was willing. I shared with her what Paul wrote in 1 Corinthians 7 about the advantages of being single and the fact that singleness was a gift from God. She was really excited that day, and a heavy burden seemed to be lifted from her shoulders.

An opposite side of the above story was evident to me in Bob. He was a talented young man and headed for the mission field. He told me that he believed it was best if he remain single. I asked him about his sexual desires. He told me that this was a serious problem which he was asking the Lord to give him victory over, but it hadn't happened yet. When I read to him from 1 Corinthians 7 and explained that a person with strong sexual desire was designed by God for marriage, he was quite surprised. When I told him that marriage was a gift from God, and that he should be thankful for the fact that God had designed him for marriage, he seemed relieved. About a year later he married a wonderful Christian girl, and he is most thankful today for that talk we had.

Jesus may have been giving a list of gifts when He referred to miraculous signs that would be performed. In Mark 16:17,18 He listed:

Casting out demons
Speaking with new tongues
Picking up snakes
Drinking deadly poison without harm
Laying hands on the sick

Comparing these words with Hebrews 2:3,4, it would appear that these are "signs and wonders, with various miracles, and gifts of the Holy Spirit."

The second and fifth miraculous signs in the list above are mentioned in 1 Corinthians 12:8-10. The other three might be placed under the general category of "miracles." "Picking up snakes" and "drinking deadly poison" are grammatically connected together with the words "it shall not hurt them." It is possible that we have a miraculous gift here of physical protection.

The "casting out demons" gift is sometimes placed by various writers in the general category of "miracles" or "faith." Because of the reference in 1 Corinthians 13:2 to "faith so that I could remove mountains" and the connection of this to casting out demons in Matthew 17:14-21, some believe that the gift of faith is the special ability from the Holy Spirit to cast out demons. We really have no way of proving this belief.

First Peter 4:10,11 seems to place all the gifts into two categories, speaking or serving, and some believe that the connection of these two verses with the previous verse, which mentions hospitality, argues for an additional gift. Such a gift would certainly be useful, and we are all familiar with people who seem to manifest hospitality in effective ways. Such people do it with joy and not reluctance.

What Conclusions Can We Make?

Don't be dogmatic! There is still much that all of us need to learn about the biblical teaching on this subject. After years of study, teaching a course on spiritual gifts to graduate school students, and holding seminars in various churches on the gifts, I'm still not convinced that any of us has the final word on spiritual gifts.

I have tried to organize the material listed above into categories that help people understand the nature and purpose of the gifts. These four categories are SPECIAL GIFTS, SPEAKING GIFTS, SERVING GIFTS, and SIGN GIFTS. I willingly confess that these categories were designed by me. It is not clear from the Bible that this is the best or the only way to organize the gifts.

SPECIAL GIFTS

In terms of church edification (Ephesians 4;11,12):

> Apostles
> Prophets
> Evangelists
> Pastor/teachers

In terms of physical desires (1 Corinthians 7:7):

> Singleness (celibacy)
> Marriage

In terms of special talents (Exodus 31:1-6; 1 Samuel 16:14-23):
> Craftsmanship
> Music

SPEAKING GIFTS (Romans 12:6,7; 1 Corinthians 12:8,10; 1 Peter 4:11)

> Prophecy (preaching)
> Teaching
> Exhortation (counseling)
> Word of Wisdom
> Word of Knowledge
> Discernment (between false and true)

SERVING GIFTS (Romans 12:7,8; 1 Corinthians 12:28; 1 Peter 4:9)

> Ministry (serving—task-oriented)
> Giving
> Leadership (motivation of people; goal-oriented)
> Showing mercy (compassion on sick and suffering)
> Helps (bringing relief to others—people-oriented)
> Administration (direction; decision-making; task-oriented)
> Hospitality

SIGN GIFTS (Mark 16:17,18; 1 Corinthians 12:8-10, 28; 13:2; Hebrews 2:3,4)

> Faith (perhaps casting out demons)
> Casting out demons (not called a gift)
> Physical protection (not called a gift)
> Gifts of healings
> Working of miracles
> Kinds of tongues
> Interpretation of tongues

To my knowledge, the gifts mentioned above comprise the total biblical list. At least it is a place to start. The Holy Spirit gives the gifts, and when we are filled with the Spirit, we will use our gifts for the glory of God and with a great deal of effectiveness and blessing to other people.

Do Spiritual Gifts Exist Today?

In spite of many books on the subject, agreement is lacking as to the necessity and use of spiritual gifts. I have found three basic viewpoints:

1. No spiritual gifts are needed today.

This viewpoint is popular among those who see the whole issue of spiritual gifts as potentially divisive and unproductive.

A pastor in the Midwest confronted me about my emphasis on spiritual gifts. He said that there was no reason to teach people that they had spiritual gifts to use for the Lord. He argued that the gifts were given at the beginning of the church, when believers were immature. Now that we have the Holy Spirit to fill us with His love and a completed Bible, we had no more need of the gifts. He gave me several good arguments, although I still do not agree with his view.

Two reasons are usually given. One deals with the argument of 1 Corinthians 12:31 and its relationship to chapter 13. Love is the more excellent way. Since it is greater than the gifts, we don't need to concern ourselves with spiritual gifts. Gifts are for the immature, in the opinion of those who hold this view. Opponents would simply answer that love makes the gifts effective but does not eliminate their necessity or use.

A second reason for eliminating spiritual gifts deals with the sufficiency of the Bible. As a complete and final revelation from God in written form, they say, why do we need gifts at all? But doesn't the Bible need to be taught? Isn't the gift of teaching still needed?

This viewpoint can be attractive to people who don't want to deal with the problems of gifts, but it certainly does not explain the differences we see in the ministries of believers in the church. Is this all related to natural talents or professional training? Some believe it is. Others of us are not convinced. Some believers appear to be gifted in areas for which they have never been trained. How do we explain this? Is there a natural talent of showing mercy? Is it merely a matter of temperament? There are too many unanswered questions. I believe that it is a good thing to encourage believers to discover and use their spiritual gifts. It shows that every believer is needed in the body of Christ, and has a special ministry from God for which he or she is responsible before God.

2. *All the spiritual gifts are for today.*

If there is no specific command to stop using the gifts, then why not argue for all of them for today? There are strong commands to "desire" the gifts (1 Corinthians 12:31 and 14:1), at least the "greater" or "best" gifts.

A good friend in the ministry feels strongly about this. He often says to me, "If the Bible doesn't say specifically to stop encouraging or using certain gifts, what makes us think that we should?"

Should we not conclude that all the gifts are needed for the church to function properly, and would not all of them continue until the second coming of Christ? This seems like the simplest and most logical viewpoint to take. Unless Scripture reveals that certain or all of the gifts have ceased to function, it would seem reasonable to assume that they all continue to exist.

This view is held by those Christians who call themselves "pentecostal" or "charismatic." While there may be some differences among them as to how many gifts are listed in the Bible, they all agree that every spiritual gift is still in operation today and should be encouraged.

3. *Certain gifts have ceased to be needed due to their unique purpose.*

This view is held by most believers who claim to be noncharismatic or nonpentecostal. Although disagreements exist as to exactly which gifts have ceased to be needed, their arguments fall into three lines of reasoning:

(a) *Apostles and prophets ceased to be needed when the Bible was completed.*

Many believers claim Ephesians 2:20 and 3:5 as proof texts for this viewpoint. They speak of apostles and prophets as the "foundation" of the church, and argue that we are not laying the foundation anymore.

They also argue that Ephesians 3:5 tells us that the revelation of God about the church which is now found in the New Testament was given to these special apostles and prophets.

This viewpoint often eliminates certain gifts that fall under the category of "sign gifts." Since the evidences of a true apostle (2 Corinthians 12:12) are "signs and wonders and mighty deeds," those gifts are eliminated with the end of the apostles' ministry.

"Sign gifts" were also used to authenticate or validate the apostles and their message from God (Mark 16:17-20 and Hebrews 2:3,4), and under this viewpoint those gifts are no longer needed now that the Bible is completed.

(b) *Miraculous sign gifts ceased to be needed when Israel was judged and devastated by the Romans.*

Those who emphasize this view point to Paul's teaching in 1 Corinthians 14:21,22 concerning tongues. They point out that tongues are a sign to unbelievers, not believers. This passage quotes from Isaiah 28:11. The "strange tongues" of that Old Testament passage refer to the ancient Assyrians. The unbelievers to whom tongues were a sign refer to the people of Israel. Tongues, therefore, were a sign to unbelieving Israel that God will judge them for their rebellion and rejection and that He will do so through the Assyrians invading the land. The Assyrians are the "tongues-speakers."

There were three occasions when this happened to Israel. Invasions that brought God's judgment were carried out by Assyria, Babylon, and Rome. Moses predicted this long ago in Deuteronomy 28:49-57. This passage was remarkably fulfilled at the time of the Roman invasion from 66-73 A.D.

(c) *Gifts of revelation ceased the moment God's revelation in written form was completed.*

As I was watching a Christian television program, the speaker said he was given a "revelation from God" right at the moment he was speaking. He then proceeded to tell the audience what it was. It involved an event mentioned in the Bible which deals with prophetic matters. The sad thing about this whole situation is that the man was really sincere and seemed dedicated to what he was doing. The only problem was that his facts were not correct, and it was embarrassing to everyone involved.

The gifts which communicate special revelation or messages from God include prophecy, word of wisdom, word of knowledge, tongues, interpretation of tongues, and discerning of spirits. Many people do not believe that these gifts are in operation today in terms of communicating revelation from God.

Those who hold this view use Hebrews 1:1,2 as evidence that the days of direct revelation are over.

These verses declare that God spoke directly to prophets in the past and "in the last of these days [literal rendering]" has spoken unto us by His Son. "These days" would refer to the days in which God spoke directly to men.

Additional proof of the end of direct revelation from God is taken from Jude 3, where we are told to "contend earnestly for the faith which was once for all delivered to the saints."

When was the faith delivered "once for all"? Those who hold this view claim that with the completion of the Bible we have no more need for direct revelation from God through the avenue of special sign gifts.

Those holding this viewpoint also point to Revelation 22:18,19:

> I testify to everyone who hears the words of the prophecy of this book: If anyone adds to these things, God will add to him the plagues that are written in this book; and if anyone takes away from the words of the book of this prophecy, God shall take away his part from the Book of Life, from the holy city, and from the things which are written in this book.

That sounds like a completed and final revelation from God!

Many people claim today that God speaks to them directly, giving additional information and direction to what we have in the Bible. Obviously such a view is difficult to deal with or to prove. We are able to check out what people say by its agreement with Scripture, but we have no way of knowing whether God spoke directly to them apart from what the Bible itself teaches.

Satan can deceive us and counterfeit the gifts. We should insist that no revelation is from God if it contradicts the plain teaching of Scripture. Most cults began and are encouraged by the visions, prophecies, and writings of their leaders, who all claim to have received direct revelation from God. Where do we draw the line?

If direct revelation from God is possible today, who is capable of determining what is from God and what is of Satan or is simply the wild imagination of finite minds? Some would answer that God gave certain believers the gift of discerning spirits for that very purpose. Others believe that it is the responsibility of pastors and church leaders to check and control these claims in the public services of the church exactly the way 1 Corinthians 14 teaches. They are responsible to rebuke false doctrine and wrong ideas.

Many believers are troubled over this issue. Because of their convictions about the Bible as a complete and final revelation from God, they simply cannot accept the reasoning that God speaks directly to people today. When people say, "God spoke to me" or "the Lord showed me in a vision," etc., they answer, "What verse?"

Most believers would agree that God speaks indirectly through the circumstances and events of our lives. God's material creation continues to speak to us of His power and greatness.

We also believe that God speaks directly to us through His Word, the Bible. We often speak of God's impressions upon our hearts when we pray. Through prayer, we believe that God speaks (like the "still, small voice" that spoke to Elijah in 1 Kings 19). However, many believers are not convinced that this is a direct revelation from God, but rather the emotional response of our hearts to what we know or want to believe about God and His will for our lives.

We all recognize that whatever is wrong about someone's claim can be exposed by biblical teaching or time

itself. For example, if someone says that God revealed to him that Jesus would return before 1980, and He did not come back by then (which obviously did not happen!), then we would say that time revealed he was wrong and mistaken about whether God had spoken to him. We could also rebuke his claim (if he was setting dates) on the basis of clear teaching in the Bible (Matthew 24:36).

All of us need to be careful about our claims. We may sincerely believe that God spoke to us, but that doesn't make it so simply because we believe it. Saying things about what God thinks, says, does, or desires is dangerous business. He is God and is not subject to our wishes and desires.

Saying What the Bible Says

Since the subject of spiritual gifts is so vitally connected to the matter of being Spirit-filled, we must be careful to say what the Bible says—no more and no less. So what does it say?

1. It speaks of spiritual gifts for every believer.
2. It does not say that craftsmanship and music are spiritual gifts.
3. It speaks about a time when certain gifts are not needed (1 Corinthians 13:8), though Christians disagree over when that time comes. Some say it refers to the second coming of Christ and others to the completion of the Bible.
4. Apostles, prophets, evangelists, and pastor/ teachers are gifted persons, not charismatic gifts.
5. Certain apostles and prophets were selected by God to receive direct revelation from God and to write Scripture. They are the foundation of the church.

6. The Bible is a completed and final revelation of God in written form.
7. The Bible does not teach that God continues to speak directly to people today, nor is it clear that He would not do so if He chose to do it.
8. Certain gifts are connected with the ministry and message of apostles and prophets, designed to authenticate or validate their message that is now found in the Bible.
9. There are apostles and prophets mentioned in the Bible who did not write Scripture.
10. There is no passage specifically telling us that we no longer have any apostles or prophets today.
11. Though certain gifts may have had a unique ministry which a completed Bible replaces, it is impossible to prove that all gifts have been so eliminated.
12. The gifts are given by the sovereign work of the Holy Spirit. They are not the result of human achievement or personal worthiness.
13. The Bible is clear that there is diversity in the distribution of the gifts, and no one gift must be demonstrated by all believers.
14. Spiritual gifts are needed today as surely as when the church began. The purposes of edification and encouragement of other believers through the use of spiritual gifts remain as the church's objectives in today's contemporary society.

The whole subject of spiritual gifts is extremely fascinating and requires a complete book in and of itself. Our purpose here is to give a basic understanding to prepare us for the discussions of the following chapters in which one of the gifts (tongues) is examined. The

reason for this is that many believers believe that the evidence of the Spirit-filled life is the ability to speak in tongues. When people ask you, "Are you Spirit-filled?" the question often implies that tongues are necessary to prove it.

Our purpose is to deal with that implication and answer it from the teaching of the Bible. The question we will be facing for the next three chapters is:

Is it necessary to speak in tongues in order to be filled with the Spirit?

5

Are Tongues
The Proof?

While sick with the flu and unable to preach in my church one Sunday, I had the opportunity to watch some of the religious programs on television. One of the speakers made the statement that the evidence of being filled with the Spirit was speaking in tongues. He said that anyone who had studied the Bible, especially the book of Acts, would conclude that tongues are the proof of both the baptism and the filling of the Holy Spirit.

He also tried to prove that speaking in tongues was not the ability to speak in known foreign languages, but in a special "heavenly language" known only to God and His angels in heaven.

I thought about all the people who might have been watching that program. Would they feel discouraged and subspiritual because they had never spoken in tongues?

The History of Tongues

Many people have never understood or experienced this matter of speaking in tongues. It sounds weird to them. Has this been a religious practice through the years? Have many people in the history of the church experienced it? What religions teach it?

The ability to speak in tongues is not limited to Christians. Before New Testament times, tongues-speaking was a common practice among various cultures and religious beliefs. The earliest record in extrabiblical history with which this writer is acquainted is an incident in 1100 B.C. An Egyptian named Wen-Amon recorded that a young man in Canaan behaved strangely and spoke in tongues. This young Canaanite was worshiping the god Ahman, an Egyptian god. Of course, the story may be just that—a story. We have no way of knowing whether such an incident actually took place.

According to history, Plato, the Greek philosopher (429-347 B.C.), referred to tongues being used in his day. He said that the prophetess of Delphi and the priestess of Dedona "spoke in strange tongues." He also said that in the temple of Baalbek, Bachian maidens of the Dionysius cult were frequently heard speaking in strange languages.

Virgil, the Greek poet who lived from 70-19 B.C., described the ecstatic speech of a priestess on the island of Delos who was worshiping the god Apollo.

Plutarch (44-117 A.D.) said that the prophetess of Delphi spoke in tongues, as was reported by Plato some 400 years previously. Lucian of Samosata (120-198 A.D.) described tongues-speaking among the worshipers of the Syrian goddess Juno.

The Gnostics, one of the early heretical groups of the Christian church, reported that many of their followers spoke in tongues. The Montanists, who taught that the Holy Spirit would descend to Phrygia and be king over the New Jerusalem, engaged frequently in tongues-speaking. Some early church leaders spoke favorably of the Montanists while others condemned them. Some regarded Montanist as being possessed by a demon and led by a deceitful spirit. The historian Eusebius says of Montanist:

> In a sort of frenzy and ecstasy he raved on and on, and he began to babble in other strange tongues.

The great church leader Tertullian was a Montanist, and he embraced speaking with tongues.

Such early church leaders as Irenaeus, Origen, Hippolytus, Ambrose of Milan, and Augustine all make references to tongues. John Chrysostom of Antioch (died 407 A.D.) refers to glossolalia (tongues-speaking) as a scriptural happening that had ceased. Peconias (292-348 A.D.), a member of a society of monks in upper Egypt, claimed to have the gift of tongues. It is also said of him that he walked on snakes and scorpions and used crocodiles for water transportation!

Augustine (354-430 A.D.), in a debate with the Donatists, said that the Holy Spirit was received without speaking in tongues. The Donatists believed that tongues were necessary. Many church historians claim that both the Montanists and the Donatists were true believers.

In the Middle Ages, not much is known except a few isolated incidents. Venerable Bede (died 735 A.D.) referred to the gift of tongues, and Thomas Aquinas (died 1247 A.D.) felt that it could be acquired by linguistic study. Several biographers say that Vincent Ferrare, a Dominican monk (1350-1419 A.D.), spoke in tongues.

A prophetess named Hildegard (1098-1179 A.D.) spoke in tongues, and many people claimed that they saw her do it. This German lady recorded her "unknown language," but out of 900 words, all of the roots, letters, and pronunciations come from either Latin or German, both of which she knew well.

The Reformation brought more conflicting viewpoints

and examples. Martin Luther said that tongues was a sign to witness to the Jews. John Calvin said that God had removed tongues from the church. Francis Xavier, a Catholic missionary (1506-1552 A.D.), is reported to have spoken in tongues.

A renewed emphasis on tongues-speaking was kindled by the Camisards, prophets in the Cevennes mountains of France around the beginning of the eighteenth century. They claimed that young children who knew only the local dialect were able to speak in perfect French while in a trance. In the same period of time the Jansenists, Roman Catholic reformers, spoke in tongues. They were opposed to justification by faith, arguing for experience as the only safe guide.

Shakerism, started by Ann Lee Stanley (died 1784 A.D.), was involved frequently in tongues-speaking. Their roots seem to go back to the Camisards in France. Ann Lee Stanley said she was the "female principle in Christ" while Jesus was the "male principle." She taught that sexual intercourse was the cause of all human corruption, and therefore condemned marriage. She instituted the practice of men and women dancing together naked, speaking in tongues at the same time. She claimed she could speak in 72 languages of the world.

In the nineteenth century a Scottish Presbyterian by the name of Edward Irving spoke in tongues. His followers were extremely interested in prophecy. Irving taught that Christ was sinful. His emphasis on the gifts of the Spirit split his church, and he started a group called the "Catholic Apostolic Church." He accepted all seven of the Catholic sacraments as well as all their ceremonies. Many reports of false prophecies and sexual immorality discredited much of their teaching and initial success.

The Mormons under Joseph Smith (died 1844 A.D.) believed and practiced speaking in tongues. Brigham Young supposedly prayed in a "pure Adamic language."

When the Salt Lake City temple was dedicated, Mormons claim that hundreds of elders simultaneously broke out in tongues-speaking.

Today, speaking in tongues is found among many false religions and cults. Witch doctors, priests, and medicine men in Haiti, Greenland, Micronesia, Africa, Australia, and Asia have claimed to speak in strange tongues. Many voodoo practitioners claim to speak in tongues. Buddhist and Shinto priests have done it, and even Moslems do it, claiming that Mohammed himself spoke in tongues.

The history of tongues is mixed. The fact that it is so prevalent among unbelievers and false religious systems adds to the confusion. It is well for us to remember that Satan always counterfeits the gifts of the Spirit.

Tongues in the Old Testament

While there is no passage clearly indicating the spiritual gift of tongues in the Old Testament, many writers see the possibility of tongues through the use of the word for "prophet" (*nabi*) or "prophesy" (*naba*). The root meaning carries the idea of "pouring forth words abundantly" or "causing to bubble up." It is sometimes translated "to rave" or "to be mad."

Some books imply the possibility of tongues in connection with the incident of Numbers 11:26-29. But the Bible does not say that it happened on this occasion.

Others point to 1 Samuel 10:5-7, where the Bible speaks of a group of prophets who met King Saul. It says that the Holy Spirit came upon them and that they were "turned into another man." What sort of change was it that would come over Saul when he would prophesy with this group of prophets? Some think that it means they spoke in tongues. The Bible does not say that, however.

First Samuel 18:10 speaks of Saul "raving" in his

house when David was playing his harp. Is this speaking in tongues? The verse indicates that an evil spirit caused it, not the Holy Spirit. Another incident in the life of Saul happened in 1 Samuel 19:20-24, but there is no proof that he spoke in tongues in this passage.

When the prophets of Baal at Mount Carmel (1 Kings 18:29) "raved," does this mean speaking in tongues? There is no way to prove it. Besides, they were unbelievers.

The conclusion? There was no tongues-speaking in Old Testament times in terms of the spiritual gift mentioned in the New Testament.

Tongues in the New Testament

The word for "tongues" (glossa) is used 50 times in the New Testament. In addition to its obvious application to the physical member in our mouths, its normal usage refers to language.

Revelation 7:9 speaks of a great multitude that comes from all "nations, tribes, peoples, and tongues." It refers to languages (cf. Revelation 14:6).

Tongues are mentioned in Mark 16, Acts 2, 10, and 19, and 1 Corinthians 12—14, referring to the spiritual gift from God as well as the practice of the church in Corinth.

The Prediction of Jesus

One gentleman asked me, "Why don't you speak in tongues? The Gospels are filled with incidents where people spoke in tongues." I felt sorry for him. Only one passage in the Gospels refers to it—Mark 16:17. Jesus predicted, "They will speak with new tongues." He called this a sign (v. 17) that "confirmed the word" (v. 20) which His apostles were to preach.

The word "new" in Mark 16:17 (kainais) is not new

from the standpoint of time, but new to the speaker. These tongues could easily be known languages of the world, but unknown to the speaker and thus miraculous.

The Day of Pentecost

Acts 2:4 tells us what happened to the 120 believers gathered in that upper room in Jerusalem:

> They were all filled with the Holy Spirit and began to speak with other tongues, as the Spirit was giving them utterance.

The word "other" (*heteros*) is "another of a different kind." They were obviously speaking in languages different from their own natural tongue. Some believe that this means an unknown or heavenly language that is absolutely different from any known languages of the world. However, Acts 2:6,8 seems to indicate otherwise. These verses say that each person heard in "his own language" (Greek *dialektos*) or his own dialect in which he was born. These verses show rather conclusively that the tongues-speaking in Acts 2 was the ability to speak in the known languages of the world without any previous knowledge of that language.

The Experience of the Gentiles

In Acts 10:44-48 Peter brings the gospel to the house of a Roman centurion named Cornelius. According to this account, the following occurred:

1. The Holy Spirit fell on them (or was poured out).
2. The Jews were amazed that the Gentiles received the gift of the Holy Spirit.
3. The Jews heard the Gentiles speaking with tongues.

4. They were baptized in water.
5. Peter said that they had received the Spirit just as he and the other Jews did.

In Acts 11:15-18 Peter recounts the story to the apostles and brethren in Jerusalem and states the following:

1. The Holy Spirit fell on the Gentiles exactly as on the Jews on the day of Pentecost.
2. It was the promised baptism of the Holy Spirit.
3. It was received at the moment of their belief in Jesus Christ.
4. The Jews concluded by this that the Gentiles were granted repentance that leads to life.

The 12 Men at Ephesus

Acts 19:1-7 tells the story of certain disciples of John the Baptist who spoke in tongues. The following facts are clear from this story:

1. Paul expected people to receive the Holy Spirit at the moment they believed.
2. They had never heard of the Holy Spirit.
3. They were baptized in water, as John the Baptist had taught.
4. They were rebaptized for their faith in Christ.
5. When the apostle Paul laid his hands on them, the Holy Spirit came on them.
6. They spoke in tongues and prophesied.

Tongues in the Book of Acts

The three occurrences listed in the book of Acts reveal the following details:

Chapter	People Involved	Place
Acts 2	120 Jews	Jerusalem
Acts 10	Gentiles	Caesarea
Acts 19	12 disciples of John	Ephesus

Many believers say that tongues also occurred in Acts 8 in the case of the Samaritans. It seems possible. Acts 8:18 says that Simon the sorcerer "saw that the Holy Spirit was bestowed through the laying on of the apostles' hands." What did he "see"? It seems possible that they spoke in tongues. There may have been other examples. We just don't know because the Bible doesn't say.

It is quite clear from Acts 10:44-48 and 11:15-18 that the Gentile experience was exactly the same as the Jewish experience. The tongues of Acts 2 are known foreign dialects. It seems logical to believe that the tongues of the Gentiles were also foreign languages. Why should Acts 19 be any different?

Acts 11:15-18 very clearly teaches that the pouring out of the Spirit (prophesied in the Old Testament), or the gift of the Holy Spirit, or the baptism of the Holy Spirit was clearly evidenced by speaking in tongues. It is also quite clear from this passage that this was proof to the Jews of the salvation of the Gentiles.

It is easy to recognize why Christians believe that the evidence of the baptism of the Holy Spirit is speaking in tongues. The record of Acts demonstrates that point. We should also recognize the association of this experience with the matter of salvation, both in the case of the Gentiles as well as the 12 disciples of John the Baptist in Acts 19.

Since the baptism of the Holy Spirit would not occur until the day of Pentecost (Acts 1:4,5), its occurrence on that day to the 120 believers in the upper room would seem to be a subsequent experience to salvation. After all, they were already believers.

In Acts 8, the receiving of the Holy Spirit (and possibly tongues as the evidence) seems a subsequent experience also, since the Samaritans had already believed the preaching of Philip.

So we have the following experiences in Acts relating to the timing of believers receiving the Holy Spirit and speaking in tongues compared to their salvation in Christ:

Acts 10 and 19—simultaneously (same oc-
    casion)
Acts 2 and 8—subsequently (days apart)

The great question about the Acts experience of tongues deals with the purpose behind it. Is the experience to be repeated every time a person believes in Christ? Obviously, many believers have never experienced it. Is the lack of a tongues experience on the part of so many believers (the majority around the world) evidence that they have not been baptized by the Holy Spirit, even though 1 Corinthians 12:13 teaches otherwise?

This is a major reason for the debate and conflict between charismatic and noncharismatic believers. Charismatics have traditionally taught that the evidence for the baptism of the Holy Spirit is speaking in tongues. You must do it at least once in order to know that you have been baptized in the Spirit.

Charismatics also teach that speaking in tongues is the evidence of being Spirit-filled. The confusion over this matter comes from Acts 2:4, which is taken to be a standard for all believers:

They were all filled with the Holy Spirit and
    began to speak with other tongues.

But would not we expect this to occur on the first day

that the Spirit began His new ministry with the body of Christ? The baptism and filling of the Spirit would of necessity occur simultaneously at the beginning.

The teaching of Ephesians 5:15-21 about being filled with the Holy Spirit makes no reference to speaking in tongues. You would think that it would have been emphasized in that passage if it were truly the evidence of being filled with the Spirit.

The record of Acts produces the following questions for our evaluation and study:

1. If the tongues of Acts are known foreign languages (unknown to the speaker), why do believers today who speak in tongues not use known foreign languages?

2. Why is there no evidence that other people spoke in tongues when believing in Jesus Christ? Should we assume that they all did even though it does not say they did?

3. Are believers who have not spoken in tongues saved? Are they baptized in the Holy Spirit? If not, how do we explain 1 Corinthians 12:13?

4. Is tongues the only evidence that one is baptized or filled with the Holy Spirit? Why doesn't God command all believers to speak in tongues if it is essential for all believers? Why does 1 Corinthians 12:30 strongly imply that some believers do not speak with tongues?

Tongues at Corinth

Outside of Mark 16:17 and the record of Acts, the only other place where we see the use of tongues in the New Testament is in 1 Corinthians 12—14.

The church at Corinth was carnal, not Spirit-filled (1 Corinthians 3:1-4). They spoke in tongues, but not all of them (1 Corinthians 12:30). They were confused about spiritual gifts and needed guidelines for the use of them in the public services of the church. Paul wrote to them in order to correct the abuses and misuse of the gifts.

The gift of tongues is mentioned in 1 Corinthians 12:10 and is called "kinds of tongues." A companion gift is also listed, called "the interpretation of tongues." Tongues are mentioned again in 1 Corinthians 12:28,30 and 13:8, and several times in chapter 14.

There are several possible viewpoints about the meaning of tongues in 1 Corinthians as it relates to the use of tongues in Acts:

1. Tongues are foreign languages unknown to the speaker (1 Corinthians and Acts).

2. Tongues are unknown languages (heavenly language or prayer language) not related to any known languages of the world (1 Corinthians and Acts).

3. Tongues in Acts are foreign languages, but in 1 Corinthians it is a heavenly or prayer language. In Acts they are the evidence of the baptism of the Holy Spirit; in 1 Corinthians they are a spiritual gift.

4. Tongues in Acts are foreign languages; tongues in 1 Corinthians include foreign languages as well as unknown languages—one the true gift and the other a counterfeit gift.

Stop and Think

Luke, who wrote Acts, was a close associate of the apostle Paul, who wrote 1 Corinthians. Doesn't it seem reasonable to conclude that they would be united on the meaning of the word "tongues"?

Also, Paul seems to make a distinction between his ability to speak in tongues and the tongues-speaking which the Corinthian church was doing (cf. 1 Corinthians 14). Is it possible that the gift of tongues was being abused and misused in Corinth? That might explain what appears to be a difference between Paul's discussion and Luke's record in Acts.

Is it not possible to conclude that the true gift of tongues was the ability to speak in known languages of the world without any previous knowledge of those languages, and that the counterfeit experience is speaking in utterances that are not intelligible, but merely some unknown combination of letters and syllables that bring an emotional release to the individual?

Could not Satan (demons) also counterfeit the true gift by causing one of his evil spirits to speak in an unknown tongue through an individual? Would that not explain the many examples of tongues-speaking among unbelievers?

What about the "interpretation of tongues"? Does this give us any clue as to the nature of tongues? The Greek word appears in different grammatical forms and is used most often to give the meaning of a person's name. The idea is that of direct translation from one language to another. It is also used in Luke 24:27, when Jesus Christ explained the things about Himself in all the Scriptures. In that context, it is not so much translation as interpretation and exposition. Our English word "hermeneutics" simply says the Greek word in English. Hermeneutics usually refers to a course of study in a Bible college or graduate school that deals with how to interpret the Bible.

Interpreting Tongues

According to 1 Corinthians 14:27, one person was able to interpret two or three speakers in tongues. If interpretation means translation, then the interpreter was simply translating known foreign languages into the language of the people present. If it means exposition or interpretation that explains the tongues-speaker's message, then it could be shorter or longer than the actual words of the tongues-speaker, depending upon what was needed to help the audience understand.

If no interpreter was present (1 Corinthians 14:28), then the tongues-speaker was to keep silent in the public assembly of the church. The reason for this is that all things are to be done for edification in the public assembly of the church. If people don't know what you are saying, then edification is impossible.

Guidelines for Tongues

Even though people know what 1 Corinthians 14 says about the use of tongues in public meetings, the guidelines are sometimes not followed. Because of the emphasis on edification of the whole church, many people today have emphasized that speaking in tongues is to be done in private for self-edification.

First Corinthians was one of the first epistles Paul wrote (around 51-52 A.D.). Those believers did not have the advantage of the whole New Testament, as we have today. Paul gave them instruction about the use of tongues, and stated the following:

1. Not all believers will speak in tongues (12:30).
2. Tongues are not as important as prophesying (14:1-5).
3. Speaking in tongues does not communicate to men, but only to God (14:2,16).
4. The tongues-speaker does not know himself what he is saying (14:2,13,14).
5. Tongues-speaking without interpretation does not edify the church (14:5,17).
6. It is more important to speak in the language of the people than in tongues (14:19).

7. To emphasize tongues above understanding and edification is a sign of immaturity (14:20).

8. Tongues are a sign to unbelievers, not believers (14:22).

9. Tongues are not for evangelism (14:23).

10. Tongues should never be used by more than three people in one service (14:27)).

11. Tongues-speakers should never speak simultaneously with each other, but rather take turns (14:27).

12. Tongues should not be used in the public meetings of the church if there is no interpreter (14:28).

13. Only one interpreter is to be used (14:27).

14. Women (wives) are not to speak in tongues in the public meetings of the church (14:34-36).

15. Tongues-speaking should not be forbidden if the guidelines are followed (14:39,40).

So should we speak in tongues?

This issue is of such importance that we have devoted the whole next chapter to it!

6

Should We Speak
In Tongues?

Many people think we should speak in tongues. Some insist on it before they will have fellowship with you. The Christians at Corinth were carnal in their attitudes and practices. Some of them (not all) could speak in tongues. Whether that was commendable or not depends on how you read Paul's instructions in 1 Corinthians chapters 12—14.

Background on the Corinthians

What was behind the trouble at Corinth in relation to spiritual gifts and tongues?

Corinth was a pagan and idolatrous city. When people became Christians they often brought their pagan ideas and practices into the church. Paul addressed this matter when he wrote in 1 Corinthians 12:1, "Now concerning spiritual gifts...." The word "gifts" is in italics because it is not in the Greek text. The basic word is "spiritualities" or "spiritual things." Paul may be referring to pagan ideas here, not spiritual gifts.

Paul discusses spiritual gifts in 1 Corinthians 12, so

why not assume that this is what he is referring to in verse 1? A look at the discussion in the opening verses suggests that Paul is dealing with pagan concepts and ideas that were brought into the church. His words "carried away to these dumb idols" clearly suggests that fact.

Paul's opening line of 1 Corinthians 12:1 could be referring to the pagan concepts of speaking in tongues. When he said, "Now concerning spiritual [things or ideas or practices]," he could have been referring to speaking in tongues as done in pagan religions. This would explain how chapter 12 is constructed and why such detail was given concerning the use of spiritual gifts in the church. It would also explain why this lengthy discussion that continues through chapter 14 was placed in the letter to the Corinthian church.

The Corinthian Practice

Though Christians differ over the interpretation of 1 Corinthians 14, there are several matters about which we all might agree.

1. *The true gift of tongues was given by the sovereign will of the Holy Spirit (1 Corinthians 12:11).*

This means that the gift of tongues cannot be gained through human initiative or intervention. Receiving a spiritual gift does not depend on human prayer or faithfulness. You either have a certain gift or you don't. Gifts are given as God wills to give, not as man wills to receive.

Mary was deeply disturbed as she shared her frustrations with me. She had been told to pray that she might be filled with the Spirit, and that this means that a person should pray to receive the gift of tongues. She tried many times, but nothing happened. She felt rejected by

God—that she could never be used by God in her life. How tragic! It was a joy to share with her the good news of the Bible's teaching on this issue. She felt relieved when she realized that whatever gift she had came from the Lord and did not depend on her own response.

2. *Every believer could not speak with tongues (1 Corinthians 12:30).*

From the standpoint of the spiritual gifts listed in 1 Corinthians 12, not all believers could speak in tongues. That's what it says! The contrary side of that would be that some believers were able to speak in tongues.

It is a terrible thing to pressure believers to speak in tongues when the Bible plainly teaches that all believers cannot do so. The possibilities for deception, rejection, bitterness, etc. are great.

I told a pastor that he was mistaken for teaching that believers must speak in tongues in order to be Spirit filled. He replied that Acts 2:4 says that all were filled and all spoke in tongues. When I asked him to explain 1 Corinthians 12:30, where it says that not all believers speak in tongues, he replied that those who don't are the carnal believers! It is a no-win situation with that kind of reasoning.

3. *The Corinthians were carnal, not Spirit-filled, and were being corrected about many things in Paul's letter to them, including tongues.*

There is really no need to argue over this point. All who love God's Word and have an appreciation for the whole context of a book know that this is true. That's what 1 Corinthians 3:1-4 clearly says about this group of believers—they were carnal, not spiritual!

Since Paul spends most of his time rebuking the Corinthians for their ideas and practices, it would seem more than likely that he is doing the same in 1 Corinthians 14 concerning tongues.

4. *The word "tongues" appears in the singular in 1 Corinthians 14 (vv. 2,4,13,14,19,26,27). It appears in the plural (tongues) in Mark 16:17, Acts, and when the true gift is listed in 1 Corinthians 12.*

A listener to my radio broadcasts wrote me about my beliefs concerning tongues. He could not understand why I believed that the Corinthian church's practice was not true to the Bible. When I pointed out to him the difference between the singular and plural forms of the word "tongues" he was amazed and told me that he had never noticed that before, though he had been teaching the Bible for many years.

That's a common problem. We can teach a certain way and believe quite strongly in our viewpoint, only to discover that we have overlooked something important in the text. That's the embarrassment that all of us who teach the Bible experience from time to time! We need to be careful about being too dogmatic.

The old King James Version of the Bible noted this problem by inserting the word "unknown" in italics in front of the singular form of the word "tongue," though it is not in the Greek text.

It is possible that the Corinthian practice of tongues (which was being corrected by Paul) is referred to by the use of the singular.

It is interesting that Paul uses the plural, "tongues," when he refers to his own use of tongues (cf. 1 Corinthians 14:14. When he refers to the proper use of the gift, he seems to use the plural (cf. 1 Corinthians 14:5,6,18,22,23,39).

The singular use of "tongue" could refer to a particular occasion or to one specific language. If the tongues-speaker was able to speak several different languages, then the singular could refer to one of those. It would appear that this might be the point behind the use of the singular in verses 26 and 27. Otherwise Paul would be encouraging the Corinthians to continue their abusive practice of the true gift! He is probably referring to the particular occasion in which one particular person used the gift.

Whether this view of the singular form of "tongue" is correct or not, it is obvious that Paul is not entirely pleased with what the Corinthians were doing.

What Was Wrong?

We are not trying to say that all tongues-speaking is categorically condemned in 1 Corinthians 14. It is not. What we are going to show is that the Corinthians were misusing the true gift. Why was their practice of tongues wrong? Paul gives us at least seven reasons.

1. *Because no one understood what the speaker was saying (1 Corinthians 14:2).*

Some believe that this point is important when using the gift in the public meetings of the church, but that it in no way restricts the use of the gift in private. They understand the statement "he who speaks in a tongue does not speak to men but to God" as being a clear reason for the use of tongues. The individual is communicating to God even though he doesn't understand what he is saying.

The last phrase of 1 Corinthians 14:2 says, "in the spirit he speaks mysteries." Some teach that the phrase "in the spirit" refers to being Spirit-filled. However, there is no definite article ("the") in front of the word "spirit" in the Greek text. There is no proof grammatically that it refers to the Holy Spirit. A more plausible argument is that it refers to the person's human spirit.

We should see this whole verse (14:2) as a correction of the Corinthian practice. They were accustomed to spiritual ecstasy at which time the "mysteries" of a particular religion were known or communicated. We believe that Paul is rebuking them for pagan ideas.

It is interesting to note that some Christians see this verse as instructive on the proper and private use of tongues. They argue that the text says he speaks "to God." How could that be true if it were merely a pagan practice?

On the other side, it could be argued that even if it were demonic influence, God would certainly know what was being communicated even if it did not make sense or was false doctrine.

But the main point is corrective. Paul is not commending the private use of tongues but showing why the Corinthian practice was wrong: because no one understands what the person is saying, and God intends that people do understand!

2. *Because the purpose of church ministry was not achieved (1 Corinthians 14:3).*

But he who prophesies speaks edification
and exhortation and comfort to men.

The word "but" would connect this verse with the preceding one. When the church gathers for its meetings, the purpose is not to use our gifts for ourselves or to display our own abilities. It is to minister to other people.

While edification builds up a person in the knowledge of God's Word, and exhortation gives direction and answers from God's Word, and comfort identifies with the person in need and shows love in the way it speaks to other people, the Corinthian practice did none of the above!

3. *Because the speaker edified only himself, not the church (1 Corinthians 14:4,5).*

> He who speaks in a tongue edifies himself, but he who prophesies edifies the church. I wish you all spoke with tongues, but even more that you prophesied; for he who prophesies is greater than he who speaks with tongues, unless indeed he interprets, that the church may receive edification.

One of the fascinating things about the differences among Christians is how we can see the exact opposite view in the same verse! Some believe in self-edification; others do not. One gentleman said to me, "But that verse (14:4) says that we edify ourselves when we speak in tongues." I replied, "But is it telling us that it is all right to do so?" He had never considered that possibility. Is it not possible that Paul is again referring to the Corinthian practice and rebuking it?

> We then who are strong ought to bear with the scruples of the weak, and not to please ourselves. Let each of us please his neighbor for his good, leading to edification. For even Christ did not please Himself (Romans 15:1-3).

Spiritual gifts were not given for self-edification but for the benefit of others. First Peter 4:10 tells us to use our gifts to "minister to one another." First Corinthians 12:7 says, "The manifestation of the Spirit is given to each one for the profit of all." Gifts are given to benefit others so that the body of Christ will function in unity and harmony.

Self-edification violates the purpose of spiritual gifts. No biblical passage teaches it. First Corinthians 14:4 does not advocate the experience of tongues for self-edification but rebukes such practice. The Corinthians were doing it, but it is not the proper use of the true spiritual gift of tongues.

4. *Because the speaker's understanding was unfruitful (1 Corinthians 14:13-15).*

A fourth reason why the Corinthian practice of tongues was wrong deals with the speaker's understanding. When Paul said in verse 14, "If I pray in a tongue," was he indicating that this is how he did it? Some people think so. Others don't. The word "if" could be translated "maybe it's true and maybe it's not." If Paul meant to say that this is what he actually did, the Greek would necessitate another word for "if" and another mood for the verb "pray." He would have to say, "If, and it is true . . ." Paul is just using himself as an illustration of what they were doing. He is not indicating what his practice actually was.

Paul points out that the problem with the Corinthian practice was that the individual's understanding was "unfruitful." To pray and sing "in the spirit" refers to the inner man. To be productive, the understanding must be there. It is never right to turn off our minds in order to have some experience! Religious experience that is divorced from mental comprehension is neither valid nor biblical.

Paul's teaching here deals with what a person feels, and it is a great statement to the fact and importance of the *mind* being the controlling factor.

I asked a tongues-speaker what he understood when he was speaking in tongues. He quickly answered, "It doesn't matter. You don't need to know." That kind of response is exactly what Paul is rebuking in these verses.

5. *Because the biblical purpose of tongues was being violated (1 Corinthians 14:20-22).*

These verses are crucial to the argument about tongues. The quotation of verse 21 is taken from Isaiah 28:11. The people speaking the foreign language in that case were the Assyrians—unbelievers!

The ones who did not listen were the people of Israel. The sign of tongues was a sign of judgment, not blessing. It was and should have been a reminder to the Jews that unless they would repent, God would bring His judgment upon them. He did so in 722 B.C., as Assyria took the ten northern tribes into captivity.

Another example is found in Jeremiah 5:14-19. God says in verse 15 that He will bring a nation against His people, and He calls them "a nation whose language you do not know, nor can you understand what they say." In this case the tongues-speakers refer to the nation of Babylon, and once again the ones who did not respond to God's message are the children of Israel, specifically the two southern tribes, Judah and Benjamin. Babylon came and destroyed Jerusalem in 586 B.C. and took the Jews into captivity.

Another example is found in Deuteronomy 28:45-50. Once again God says that He will bring a "nation whose language you will not understand" against His people of Israel if they do not obey Him. Many teachers believe that this passage was fulfilled in the invasion of Rome. The details fit the Roman destruction of 70 A.D.

Tongues were a sign, but not to believers. According to the apostle Paul, tongues were a sign of the removal of national blessing upon Israel and the coming of the blessing of God upon all nations and languages. The outpouring of the Holy Spirit, which was prophesied several times in the Old Testament and was referred to by Peter in his message on the day of Pentecost in Acts 2, refers to the salvation of both Jews and Gentiles. The great event and the subsequent rejection of Israel were announced and declared by the presence of tongues.

Tongues, therefore, were primarily a sign to unbelieving Israel and a warning of coming judgment if they
refused to repent. This would also explain the purpose
of tongues in confirming the message of the apostles
which announced God's message and exhorted God's
people to repent and believe the gospel.

6. *Because the results upon unbelievers were not good
   (1 Corinthians 14:23-25).*

Another reason why the Corinthian practice was
wrong was because of the effect which tongues-speaking
had upon unbelievers who visited the assembly of the
Christians. Paul says that unbelievers would say of
tongues-speakers, "You are out of your mind (v. 23)."
If there is no interpretation, how would unbelievers (or
believers, for that matter) know what was being said?

A couple who claimed to speak in tongues heard my
teaching on 1 Corinthians 14 and were greatly concerned. They commented after my message, "We
thought our speaking in tongues was a testimony and
witness to nonbelievers who might be in the audience.
But it has bothered us at times when we wondered how
they would know what we were saying, especially when
there was no interpretation." Exactly.

7. *Because all were trying to be involved in the public
   assembly (1 Corinthians 14:26-40).*

This extended passage about the use of tongues in
the public meetings of the church is very vital to our
understanding about what was taking place in Corinth.
Their pagan ideas and practices were controlling the
services of the church. Paul wrote these guidelines to
confront the Corinthians. Each point was a direct rebuke
of very commonly held opinions in the mystery and cultic
religions of Corinth.

The key phrase is found in verse 26: "*Whenever you come together.*"

Paul is talking about the use of tongues in the public meetings of the church. He is not condemning all usage of tongues. He is merely teaching how to use tongues and other gifts in a proper way, one that glorifies the Lord and edifies His church.

A lady wrote me a lengthy letter concerning the practice of tongues in her church. She had been reading 1 Corinthians 14 and was concerned about its application in her experience. She did not mind people using the gift of tongues in private, but it was the public display that concerned her. She wanted to know why Paul was controlling the use of tongues and what exactly he meant in the closing verse of 1 Corinthians 14. I told her that Paul gave three reasons as to why the Corinthian practice in the public meetings was wrong.

1. *Because it leads to confusion (v. 33) and disorder (v. 40).*
2. *Because it causes some believers to violate the Scriptures (vv. 34-36).*
3. *Because it results in spiritual pride and ignorance (vv. 37,38).*

Why the Confusion?

When everyone tries to be involved in one meeting, it produces chaos, not blessing. Chaotic religious meetings were common among pagan cultures. It was expected. No one cared about anyone besides himself. This is the way of Satan, not God. God is a God of order and decency.

When every person can do whatever he wants to in a public meeting, it reveals a lack of leadership and a lack of confidence in the God of the Bible. Some believers view an order of service with suspicion. They think it quenches the work of the Holy Spirit. But why can't the Spirit lead some people to plan the service and the gifts of people in an orderly manner? Is there not a gift of leadership and administration also? Of course.

Why Violate Scripture?

A special problem in 1 Corinthians 14 deals with women. The Greek word for "women" can also refer to wives, and that is what is meant in verses 34-36. Verse 35 says that if these women (wives) want to learn anything they are to "ask their own husbands at home." Obviously wives are intended, not women in general. The problem here deals with the relationship of a wife to her husband, not a criticism of women ministering in the church.

In the kind of meetings which went on in Corinth, wives were freely involving themselves. Knowing the customs of Corinth's culture and religious thinking in that day, they were conducting themselves in a manner which did not reflect their submission to their husbands, but rather displayed emotions and outbursts that would be embarrassing to their husbands and children.

The primary issue is that of a wife's relationship to her husband. The Bible teaches that both men and women were involved in the ministries of the church, but there are strong words directed to wives concerning the danger of usurping their husbands' authority and leadership (cf. 1 Timothy 2:11-15).

Why Spiritual Pride?

A third reason behind Paul's attention to certain guidelines for the use of tongues in the public meetings of the church deals with the problem of pride. First Corinthians 14:37,38 says:

If anyone thinks himself to be a prophet or
spiritual, let him acknowledge that the things
which I write to you are the commandments
of the Lord. But if anyone is ignorant, let him
be ignorant.

It is possible that the apostle Paul is using satire here.
Many so-called "spiritual" ones felt and acted superior
to others. They believed that they were more knowl-
edgeable. Paul's point is that if anyone did not obey his
instructions about the public meetings of the church, it
would be proof that his claims were false.

What About 1 Corinthians 14?

It is only right that we present the viewpoints of those
who see 1 Corinthians 14 as a commendation rather
than a condemnation of tongues. The argument would
go something like this (based upon charismatic lit-
erature):

1. We are speaking to God only, and therefore it
   is not necessary for us to understand what we
   are saying (14:2,28).
2. We are speaking in our spirit, and that is good
   for us because it releases us from an intellectual
   approach that confines and limits what we can
   experience (14:2).
3. We are edifying ourselves, and there is nothing
   wrong with that (14:4).
4. Paul wants us all to speak with tongues (14:5).
5. We are praying in the spirit, and Paul says that
   this is right for us to do (14:14,15).
6. Paul spoke in tongues; why shouldn't we
   (14:18)?
7. Paul says that a person with a "tongue" has a
   place in the ministry of the church (14:26).

8. Paul says that people can speak (two or three) in tongues if there is an interpreter present (14:28).
9. Paul says that we are not to forbid speaking in tongues (14:39).

Many believers feel that enough is said in 1 Corinthians 14 to prove the validity and practice of tongues for today. Others, of course, do not agree. While they may accept the legitimate use of tongues, based on its biblical purpose and stated duration, they believe that current practices are often duplications of the Corinthians' practice which Paul condemned.

Should We Speak in Tongues?

The experiences in Acts are unusual and distinct in terms of God's purposes. They demonstrate the beginning of a new work of the Holy Spirit which will result in the salvation of multitudes of Gentiles. They are not repeated.

The teaching of 1 Corinthians is that there is a spiritual gift of speaking in tongues given to a few believers, but not to all. It had a specific purpose. It could be easily counterfeited by carnal believers or unbelievers.

Is the true gift still being used today? That's the bottom line! If the true gift is the ability to speak in foreign languages without any previous knowledge of those languages, then we must answer no. The majority of those who claim to speak in tongues do not speak in known foreign languages of the world.

If the true gift is an unknown "heavenly language" or "prayer language," is it being used today? There is no way to prove it. In spite of claims to the contrary, a person's experience is the only criterion. How can we know if a group of unrelated letters and syllables is being given by the Holy Spirit? It could be divine in origin, or it could be psychological, emotional, or even satanic.

7

Are Tongues
For Today?

Many Christians believe that you must speak in
tongues in order to be filled with the Spirit. This is the
major view of charismatics. This is what it means to be
charismatic: You believe that speaking in tongues is a
gift which all believers can exercise and in fact must be
done in order to be baptized or filled with the Holy Spirit.
It is the evidence which charismatics are looking for when
they speak of being Spirit-filled.

John, a charismatic teacher, insisted that I speak in
tongues. He said that if I were willing to do it, it would
happen to me. I questioned that belief. I might be willing
to sell my soul to the devil, but that would not make
it right! The issue is not my willingness, but whether the
Bible teaches it. I don't want any experience that is
forbidden by God, nor do I want to pursue an experience that is not commanded by God for all believers.

Mary was sincere. Friends told her that she should
speak in tongues if she wanted to be filled with the Spirit.
They laid hands on her and prayed very emotionally
that it would happen. They encouraged her to just open

her mouth and let the words pour forth. The words did not come.

After several frustrating attempts, they accused her of a lack of faith, and that there must be something in her life that was quenching the Spirit. She didn't know of anything, but they began to pray that whatever demon was inside her would now come out so she could be released to speak in tongues. Again, nothing happened. The people left, believing that she was guilty of something but simply unwilling to confess it.

After this horrible experience, she came to see me. She was hurt, depressed, and feeling guilty for her lack of faith. I then shared with her what the Bible teaches about the filling of the Spirit as well as the matter of speaking in tongues. She began to gain confidence through the Word of God and is now growing in her faith and experiencing the joy of her Christian life. She was fortunate; others I have talked with have not been able to escape the feelings of failure and defeat which such an experience often brings.

The Three Main Issues

1. Are tongues the proof? (Chapter 5)
2. Should we speak in tongues? (Chapter 6)
3. Are tongues for today? (Chapter 7)

The first question deals with the nature and practice of tongues. The second question deals with the purpose of tongues and the problem of tongues in the church at Corinth. The final question deals with the future. Are tongues to be practiced by the church throughout its history until Jesus comes? Does the Bible indicate the duration of tongues?

A key verse on the subject of the duration of tongues is found in 1 Corinthians 13:8:

> Love never fails. But whether there are
> prophecies, they will fail; whether there are
> tongues, they will cease; whether there is
> knowledge, it will vanish away.

The key phrase in that verse is "... tongues, they will cease."

When tongues will come to an abrupt stop is the major issue dealing with the use and purpose of tongues today.

A Look at the Context

First Corinthians 13 continues the discussion of chapter 12 about spiritual gifts, pointing out the necessity of love in using the gifts and the superiority of love over the use of gifts. Gifts will one day fail, but love never will. First Corinthians 13:8-13 reads:

> Love never fails. But whether there are
> prophecies, they will fail; whether there are
> tongues, they will cease; whether there is
> knowledge, it will vanish away. For we know
> in part and we prophesy in part. But when
> that which is perfect has come, then that
> which is in part will be done away. When I
> was a child, I spoke as a child, I understood
> as a child, I thought as a child; but when I
> became a man, I put away childish things. For
> now we see in a mirror, dimly, but then face
> to face. Now I know in part, but then I shall
> know just as I also am known. And now abide
> faith, hope, love, these three; but the greatest
> of these is love.

Gifts, as wonderful as they are, will not last forever—love will! The desire for spiritual gifts is proper (1 Corinthians 14:1), but gifts are not to be the highest pursuit of the believer. Next to glorifying God (1 Corinthians 10:31), the believer's highest pursuit is to love God and other people.

Jesus said to a lawyer who asked about the greatest commandment of all:

> You shall love the Lord your God with all your heart, with all your soul, and with all your mind.

Jesus said that this was the greatest commandment of all, and that the second-greatest was just like it:

> You shall love your neighbor as yourself.

Spiritual gifts are greatly misunderstood and abused. They are wonderful blessings when God's love is controlling, but they can become curses when His love is absent! Love is more important than spiritual gifts, but it takes a measure of maturity and growth to know the reason why.

Ed is a good Bible teacher, and every person who has heard him teach speaks of his gift. His Sunday school class was growing, and from all outward signs his gift was being greatly used of the Lord. Then everything went bad. He became critical and judgmental of other people. People started to leave his class to go to other classes. What was wrong? It was a simple problem, but hard to detect at first: The love of God was missing. Without God's love, his gift was hurting instead of edifying. Love is our greatest need in ministry!

Love Never Fails

The key phrase to 1 Corinthians 13:8-13 is "Love never fails." The Greek reads literally, "*The* love never at any point of time is failing." It never fails to be effective or to accomplish things. It never lacks force or power. It always works! Other good things (such as spiritual gifts) can fail, both in time and under certain circumstances. God's love never fails! We need it more than anything else in our lives.

He was a missionary, but experiencing great conflicts in his relationship with other people. He had served the Lord faithfully for over 25 years, but things were not going well on the field. He loved the Lord and wanted to serve Him. What was wrong? In our conversations, the matter of God's love came up. He was immediately convicted. He had strong convictions and knew all the right answers. He had just one problem—a lack of love. His ministry was being hurt because of this one thing. How desperate is our need for love! It takes years for many of us to learn this lesson. I was so glad to see this missionary respond. Because of what has happened to him in terms of experiencing and manifesting God's love, his ministry is now being blessed mightily of the Lord. Praise the Lord for His love!

To illustrate the unfailing nature of love and its absolute importance to our lives and ministries, the apostle Paul reveals the temporary nature of certain gifts.

He mentions three gifts, or literally the results of three gifts, in 1 Corinthians 13:8. The word "whether" can be translated "if at this point in time, and it is so." In other words, there is no doubt about the existence of these gifts. Our English word "since" fits the idea of this Greek phrase. We could translate, "since at this point in time there are prophecies. . . ." At the writing of 1 Corinthians the gifts of prophecy, tongues, and knowledge were definitely in operation.

When commenting on prophecy and knowledge, Paul uses the exact same verb in Greek, though translated in English by different words. In the New King James Version, the words "will fail" and "will vanish away" come from the exact same verb in Greek. The word suggests a phasing out over a period of time. It can be translated "to render inoperative" or "to become ineffective." According to Paul, the gifts of prophecy and knowledge would be phased out or gradually eliminated.

Not so with tongues.

When Paul refers to tongues, he changes the words and says that "they will cease" or come to an abrupt stop. In contrast with the phasing-out process of prophecies and knowledge, tongues will continue until a certain point in time, and then immediately stop.

Another interesting fact about 1 Corinthians 13:8 is that the word for "prophecy" is in the plural, and should be translated "prophecies." It is referring to content, not proclamation. The result of the gift of prophecy is "prophecies." The word "knowledge" is, of course, in the singular, as it always is (no such word as "knowledges").

At the writing of 1 Corinthians (one of the earliest of the epistles of Paul), prophecies and knowledge were serving an important purpose, as well as tongues. But something better was coming which would eliminate the need for prophecies, knowledge, and tongues.

Prophecies and Knowledge

Both prophecies and knowledge refer to revelation from God—the communication of God's words. At the time of 1 Corinthians, the revelation of God which we now find in the New Testament was incomplete. A portion of what the New Testament now contains had been put into writing by the time Paul wrote this letter to Corinth. There was a great deal more to follow, much of which would be revealed by Paul, and some by John, James, Jude, and Peter.

Tongues were needed as long as the revelation of God was being communicated through the apostles and prophets. They were a part of the signs which God used to confirm or authenticate the ministry and message of these men of God who wrote the books of the New Testament (Mark 16:17-20; Hebrews 2:1-4).

If you read 1 Corinthians carefully, you discover that the point in time at which "prophecies" and "knowledge" will be phased out is the same time at which "tongues" will cease to exist. Naturally, the great debate is over the point in time when this would occur!

If tongues are still in operation today (as many claim), then prophecies and knowledge are still being communicated to men. Many Christians believe that this in fact is the case. They speak about how God speaks to them and reveals things.

Such a position is dangerous. Can we add new revelation to what is contained in the 66 books of the Bible? Many cultic groups think so, and that is why they have additional revelation which they treat with honor and respect equal to the Bible itself. It is an understandable position if you believe that God continues to reveal things directly to men today. But does He do that?

The Complete Revelation

Jude 3 indicates that the point in time of God's revelation being spoken to man had already come:

> Beloved, while I was very diligent to write
> to you concerning our common salvation, I
> found it necessary to write to you exhorting
> you to contend earnestly for the faith which
> was once for all delivered to the saints.

How would we know when the last book in the process had arrived? Would there always be a problem in church history of additional books? Should we be looking for that final book, or is it already here?

The answer is found in the last book of the Bible, the

book of Revelation. In chapter 22 (the last chapter), verses 18 and 19, we find some very important words dealing with the issue of God's revelation being completed:

> I testify to everyone who hears the words of the prophecy of this book: If anyone adds to these things, God will add to him the plagues that are written in this book; and if anyone takes away from the words of the book of this prophecy, God shall take away his part from the Book of Life, from the holy city, and from the things which are written in this book.

Some people argue that Revelation 22:18,19 is only to be applied to the book of Revelation, and not to the entire Bible. However, consider for a moment the contents of the book of Revelation. They deal with future events (at least from chapter 4 on) all the way into the eternal state. How can you add anything to that? All that God will do in the future has been recorded. No one can add to it or take away from it without experiencing serious consequences!

The purpose of tongues (1 Corinthians 14:22) is that they are "for a sign, not to those who believe, but to unbelievers." In 1 Corinthians 14:21 we have a quotation from Isaiah 28:11. The people of Israel were not responding to God's revelation, and God used tongues (the language of the Assyrians, who would bring God's judgment upon them, which happened in 722 B.C.) to confirm the authority and accuracy of His revelation to them through the prophets.

As long as God was giving new revelation through His apostles and prophets (cf. Ephesians 2:20 and 3:5), tongues were needed to authenticate them and their message. The gifts of prophecy, knowledge, and tongues were temporary gifts. A point in time was coming in which they would no longer be needed. A point in time was coming when God's revelation would be completed!

The Passing Gifts

There are two basic reasons that Paul gives in his arguments in 1 Corinthians 13:8-13:

1. *Because they give only partial understanding.*
2. *Because something is coming that will bring complete understanding.*

In 1 Corinthians 13:9 Paul wrote, "For we know in part and we prophesy in part."

Paul realized that he (in spite of the abundance of revelation given to him—cf. 2 Corinthians 12) did not have the complete truth. He had only partial understanding. As he wrote 1 Corinthians, it was not complete—there was more coming.

In 1 Corinthians 13:10 Paul said:

When that which is perfect has come, then
that which is in part will be done away.

What is "that which is in part"? Obviously it refers to "prophecies" and "knowledge," according to verse 9. That which is coming is called "perfect." What is meant by "perfect"?

The Greek word is used about 75 times in the New Testament in its various forms. About four major ideas are connected with the usage of this word.

(a) *It is used of that which is whole or complete.*

It means that nothing is left out. It is used of sacrifices that are without blemish. God's love is called "perfect" in 1 John 4:18. Perfect love doesn't lack anything. In that passage, love has no room for fear.

Matthew 5:48 tells us to be "perfect" as our heavenly Father is perfect. It is referring to the matter of loving our enemies. In order for us to be complete or total in our love, we must love our enemies as well as our friends.

(b) *It is used for maturity.*

The Greek philosophers (such as Plato and Aristotle) used this Greek word when referring to the end of the learning process. It meant that there was no need for further advancement. The Bible uses it in that way in Colossians 1:28.

(c) *It is used for biological growth.*

It refers to that which is full-grown. In the case of people, it is the word for adults. It is used of animals as well as humans, and is the opposite of children and youth. Adults are capable of reproduction and are called "perfect" or "full-grown." First Corinthians 14:20 appears to use this concept of the word when it says:

> Brethren, do not be children in understanding; however, in malice be babes, but in understanding be *mature*.

(d) *It is used of completing a task.*

In Acts 20:24 Paul spoke about his desire to "finish my race." He wanted to be faithful to God in fulfilling God's purpose for his life. Jesus said in John 4:34 that He wanted to "finish His work" (cf. John 17:4).

Whatever the "perfect" is, it is the same in nature or substance as that which is "in part." The partial is a part of the perfect, or the completed thing. That which is partial is described in 1 Corinthians 13:9 as being knowledge and prophecies—in other words, the revelation from God. It seems only logical to believe that the "perfect" thing which is coming refers to the revelation of God as well.

The perfect thing which is coming is the completion of God's revelation to man. When it comes, the gifts that have given us new revelation from God (prophecy and knowledge) would be phased out. They were continually being phased out with the writing of each New Testament book. The process would be completed with the writing of the final New Testament book. Conclusion: *The perfect thing refers to the completed Bible!*

James 1:22-25 concurs with this view when it says:

> Be doers of the word, and not hearers only, deceiving yourselves. For if anyone is a hearer of the word and not a doer, he is like a man observing his natural face in a mirror; for he observes himself, goes away, and immediately forgets what kind of man he was. But he who looks into the *perfect* law of liberty and continues in it, and is not a forgetful hearer but a doer of the word, this one will be blessed in what he does.

The use of the mirror as an illustration reminds us of 1 Corinthians 13:12. The word "perfect" is used in James 1:25 as an adjective modifying the word "law"—obviously referring to God's Word. God's Word is complete.

Psalm 119:89 reminds us, "Forever, O Lord, Your word is settled in heaven." God's revelation (its final and complete form communicated to man) was settled long ago in heaven before it was ever given to men. If God did not want to put a stamp of finality on His written Word, He easily could have eliminated Revelation 22:18,19!

As wonderful as God's revelation (the "perfect" thing) is, and as marvelous as the gifts for communicating it (prophecy, knowledge, tongues) are, love is greater because it will never fail!

We are glad for everyone who discovers spiritual gifts and uses them for the glory of God and the building up of His church. But never forget that love is greater than any gift. Love is eternal—it never fails. Gifts are temporary (regardless of your viewpoint as to how long they are needed!). In all of our efforts to discover spiritual gifts, never should we neglect the love of God. It is more important than any gift. Without God's love, our spiritual gifts are ineffective in the building up of other believers. God's love is what builds people up (cf. 1 Corinthians 8:1; Ephesians 4:16).

First Corinthians 13:11 says:

> When I was a child, I spoke as a child, I understood as a child, I thought as a child; but when I became a man, I put away childish things.

Why do things not last forever? Because we grow up! The words "put away" in verse 11 are the same words as in verses 8 and 10. The "things" of the child refer to prophecies and knowledge, that which is "partial" and not "perfect." They are lacking in complete understanding, like the child.

God's love is the way of maturity. Knowledge, understanding, and spiritual gifts used by an individual can reflect immaturity when God's love is absent.

The "perfect" thing (God's complete revelation) gives us understanding about God's love and God's ways that produces a mature, loving lifestyle. God's love never fails. Spiritual gifts will run their course; they are temporary when compared with the love of God.

Other Views

Some Bible teachers believe that the perfect thing is love itself. There is reason for this. First John 4:18 speaks of perfect love. However, the perfect thing in 1 Corinthians 13:10 had not yet arrived at the writing of 1 Corinthians. God's love was certainly available at that time.

Many believers insist that the perfect thing refers to Jesus Christ at His second coming. They are especially influenced by the phrase "face to face" in verse 12.

The adjective "perfect" in 1 Corinthians 13:10 is neuter rather than masculine, which makes it difficult to apply to the Person of Jesus Christ. Some respond to this by saying that it refers to the *event* of His second coming, not the Person. However, this is hard to reconcile with the interpretation of "face to face."

Some teachers believe that the word "perfect" applies to the future millennial age or the eternal state. There is a lack of biblical usage to prove this point, but it is certainly a possibility.

Some argue that the word "perfect" applies to the body of Christ. First Corinthians 12 does speak about the body with its many members. Under this viewpoint, the gifts would continue until the body of Christ is completed, obviously at the end of the age.

Others believe that the "perfect" thing refers to Paul's usage in Ephesians 4:13 and means maturity. The problem here is in determining whether that maturity is the maturity of the individual believer or the corporate body of believers, and if so, when can we say that this maturity has come?

In spite of the good points in other views, it still seems to this writer that the best and most consistent view with other Scripture is that the "perfect" thing refers to God's complete revelation in written form—namely, the Bible.

The obvious identification with the partial (prophecies and knowledge) seems to give strong support to this view. So does the use of the "mirror" in 1 Corinthians 13:12, especially when connected with other passages such as 2 Corinthians 3:18 and James 1:22-25. The obvious use of the word "perfect" in James 1:25 when it refers to God's Word is also a powerful argument.

Mirror Versus Face-to-Face

The tendency of the Corinthians was spiritual pride over their knowledge and their gifts. Paul's argument in chapter 13 is that the gifts are temporary and that their present knowledge was incomplete—there was more coming than what they presently had available to them. They were pursuing the wrong things—knowledge and gifts. First Corinthians 14:1 tells them to "pursue love."

Desiring (being enthusiastic or zealous about) spiritual gifts was fine, especially when the believers knew the importance of certain gifts (like prophecy—chapter 14), but God's love was the greatest thing of all. It never fails. Their present knowledge was incomplete, and their use of gifts would not last, but God's love was permanent and eternal.

One day a young man with a great desire to teach God's Word came into my office to talk with me. He had many talents and was a good student of God's Word. His ability to teach at his age was far superior to mine when I was his age. I marveled at his gift and his understanding. But he had a problem: People were not responding to his teaching. He asked me why. I asked him, "Do you love the people you are teaching?" He was taken back by the question, and spent a few moments reflecting on it. Then he replied, "Thanks. I needed that reminder. Without love we are nothing." He was teachable. I learned a great lesson from him on that score!

No matter how great your gifts are, without God's love you will fail. But love never fails.

Paul makes two statements about the present understanding of the Corinthians:

1. "Now we see in a mirror dimly."
2. "Now I know in part."

The use of the word "mirror" appears only here and in James 1:25. The word "dimly" (the English word "enigma" comes directly from the Greek word) means "in obscurity." Things are now like riddles, Paul says. We don't see everything properly or correctly. The Lord said about Moses in Numbers 12:8:

I speak with him face to face, even plainly,
and not in dark sayings.

In 1 Corinthians 13, Paul was probably quoting from this passage. The Lord said that He would make Himself known to Moses. There would be no obscurity in His communication with Moses. At the time Paul wrote 1 Corinthians, the knowledge they had was often "obscure." It was not completely clear.

When Paul said "Now I know in part," he was indicating that even though his knowledge was far superior to that of the Corinthians, it was still not complete. It would be years after his death that God would finally bring an end to His revelation to men (about 95 A.D., when John wrote Revelation).

No matter what you know or do not know, without

God's love you will not be effective in ministry to other people. Today we have a complete written revelation from God to men to study. But the need for God's love is just as strong in our lives today as it was when Paul wrote 1 Corinthians! God's love will continue forever. There is always room to grow in understanding and experiencing the love of God..

We will not always know everything we would like to know, nor settle matters that we would like to settle. But we can always experience and exercise a little more of God's love. There are some things that we will never understand until we get to heaven!

When Paul spoke about future understanding, he said two things also:

1. "Face to face."
2. "Then I shall know just as I also am known."

The "face-to-face" phrase could refer to being in heaven and seeing the Lord face to face. Our knowledge then will certainly be superior to what it is now. However, this phrase could also be referring to the complete revelation of God in written form—the "perfect" thing that is coming and now (today) has come. Verse 12 says "*then* face to face."

This phrase should be connected with the word "mirror." "Face to face" is how we look into a mirror. At the time of writing 1 Corinthians, things were not clear. They saw in the "mirror dimly." But when the entire New Testament would be completed, they would see clearly, or "face to face."

The phrase "but then I shall know just as I also am known" could refer to being in heaven with the Lord, or it could refer to God's complete revelation in written form. A complete, full understanding of the plan of God is found in the Scriptures. It was not complete when 1

Corinthians was written, but by the end of the first century A.D. it was.

The words "just as I also am known" refer to God's knowledge of Paul in terms of his salvation. Paul's knowledge would be brought up to that particular level of understanding when the Word of God was completed. Naturally, there will be much more to learn in eternity! Even those who believe that this full knowledge is not the written Word of God but future heavenly knowledge will admit that we will continue to learn and to know things forever and ever!

Though many views are given on these verses in 1 Corinthians 13:8-13, one thing remains clear to all: God's love will not fail! When certain gifts are no longer needed, and knowledge is finally complete, God's love will still be there, still needed! Your greatest need is still God's love, and always will be.

Tongues Today?

Is the gift of tongues still here today? The purpose of tongues has run its course. The need for tongues no longer exists. We have a complete and final revelation from God to men in written form — the Bible. But even if this view is incorrect, the issue of tongues is still a secondary one to the fulfillment of the Great Commission and the authority of God's Word, the Bible. Also, even if the gift of speaking in tongues were still needed today, it would be relegated by the Word of God to a secondary position when compared to prophecy (proclaiming God's Word, the Bible), and cannot be compared in value to the love of God, which all of us desperately need in our lives and ministries.

What About Being Spirit-Filled?

It is impossible to prove that speaking in tongues is

the evidence of the Spirit-filled life. Since the gift of tongues was used by a carnal church, it is no proof that the individual who does speak in tongues is filled with the Spirit.

Also, it is clear according to 1 Corinthians 12:30 that all believers do not have the gift of tongues. Even if the gift of tongues were with us today, it would be unscriptural to teach that all believers must speak in tongues in order to demonstrate that they are filled with the Holy Spirit.

8

What Hinders
The Spirit?

The Holy Spirit is God, but He never forces Himself upon us. He does not drag us to discipleship. He draws us by His love. We are not robots; we can resist the Spirit just as we resist other people. God could have made things differently, but He didn't. He gave us a will to choose, and with it we can choose either good or evil. Therefore we are responsible and accountable for our actions.

The man in my office was defeated—so discouraged that he felt there was no hope for him. He heard much about the power of the Holy Spirit and being Spirit-filled, but those ideas had no impact on his life. He had come to believe that it was a doctrine that Christians had concocted to make themselves feel better or to escape from the realities of life.

I reviewed with him some of the reasons why the Holy Spirit's presence and power may not be felt or working in his life. He seemed surprised. After sharing a few minutes with him, he responded, "I'm guilty on all the points you have mentioned!" I stopped and asked him if he wanted to do something about it. Fortunately he said yes. Things really changed for this man in the months that followed. He had a new joy and enthusiasm for the Lord about which many other people commented.

We don't often hear about the sins we can commit against the Holy Spirit, but it is crucial to understand these hindrances to being Spirit-filled. They explain why people are often defeated and discouraged in their Christian lives. When we confess and forsake these hindrances, the Holy Spirit's power is released within us.

How Unbelievers Resist the Holy Spirit

Before we discuss the unique problems which *believers* have in hindering the work of the Holy Spirit, it is important for us to see how *unbelievers* resist the Spirit.

Jesus spoke of the power of human volition when He said in Matthew 23:37:

> O Jerusalem, Jerusalem, the one who kills the prophets and stones those who are sent to her! How often I wanted to gather your children together, as a hen gathers her chicks under her wings, *but you were not willing!*

The power of human resistance to the love of God is amazing indeed! Only the depravity of the human heart can explain man's refusal to accept God's kindness and grace.

The gentleman who confronted me after church one Sunday morning was upset over what I had said about the ability of man to resist the grace of God. He spoke for several minutes to me of the irresistible grace of God. There was much that he said with which I could agree. However, he had one fallacy: He did not see the extent of man's depravity. We often resist the lovingkindness of God even though it is frequently manifested to us. This man was sincere in his beliefs. He felt that God could not be resisted because He is God. Of course, if God wanted to match His power against us, there would be no contest! But the Bible indicates that God has given man the ability to choose.

As I sat under a beautiful tree outside my dormitory room in college, I was trying to comprehend the dilemma which my theology professor had just laid on our class. He said that the sovereignty of God and the responsibility of man were like two parallel lines that never intersect in our finite minds. Both are true, and are only apparently contradictory because of our human limitations. It sounded good, but I decided to try to bring those two lines together and explain it all in simple terms. Now, years later, I think I need to sit down again under that tree!

What the Bible Teaches

When all else fails, read the directions! In the Bible there are at least four ways in which the unbeliever can resist the Holy Spirit of God.

1. *By failing to obey God.*

This point is clearly brought out by Stephen in Acts 7:39,51. According to Acts 6:15, he was confronting the Sanhedrin (council), the highest political and religious body of Israel. The high priest inquired about the truthfulness of the accusations against him, and he replied with a lengthy message dealing with the history of Israel.

He said in Acts 7:39 that the fathers of Israel "rejected" the Lord, specifically stating that they "would not obey." In verse 51 he called them "stiffnecked and uncircumcised in heart and ears." These terms refer to unbelievers. He then said, "You always resist the Holy Spirit." There it is—unbelievers can resist the Holy Spirit by refusing to obey the Lord.

Their response to his arguments was not too pleasant. They "gnashed at him with their teeth" (v. 54) and eventually stoned him (v. 58). Obviously their reactions demonstrated that they were unbelievers. An interesting contrast is made between them and Stephen. Stephen was declared to be "full of the Holy Spirit" (v. 55). They were full of anger, but not the Holy Spirit. Their refusal to obey God proved that they were resisting the Holy Spirit.

2. By failing to accept God's grace and forgiveness.

This is a simple but powerful point. Hebrews 10:26-31 is a discussion about people who sin willfully. They know what God says about a sacrifice for sin, but they refuse to bring one.

Verse 28 says that a person who sins willfully has rejected Moses' law. The writer of Hebrews then applies this Old Testament teaching to the present generation and says in verse 29:

> Of how much worse punishment, do you suppose, will he be thought worthy who has trampled the Son of God underfoot, counted the blood of the covenant by which he was sanctified a common thing, and insulted the Spirit of grace?

When Jesus Christ died on the cross, He was the final sacrifice for sin. There is no other sacrifice that will atone for our sin. If we treat this matter lightly and do not accept His forgiveness and His death on the cross for our sins, we have "insulted the Spirit of grace." The Holy Spirit is characterized by grace, which gives us what we do not deserve—namely, salvation from our sins through the work of Jesus Christ on the cross.

If a person refuses to accept the sacrifice of Christ, there is no hope, and because of insulting the Holy Spirit, who is extending grace and love to us through Jesus Christ, we will be lost forever, and deserve to be so!

After reading that passage in Hebrews to a man one day and explaining the meaning of it, he was deeply moved. He said to me, "I had no idea that I was insulting God!" Yet his refusal to accept the death of Jesus Christ as his only sacrifice for his sins was exactly that—an insult to God the Holy Spirit. His heart was moved by the gravity of his sin, and he prayed that day to trust Jesus Christ as his only Savior from sin. Have you made that commitment?

3. *By failing to tell the truth.*

There is quite a revealing story in the book of Acts about two people who claimed to be believers but were deceitful and dishonest. The story, in Acts 5:1-11, deals with a couple named Ananias and Sapphira. They sold a piece of land and gave some of the money to the church to help other believers, but then lied about the total price they received. They kept back a part of it (which they had a right to do) but wanted the church to believe that they had given all the money.

The apostle Peter confronted them and said (Acts 5:3,4):

> Ananias, why has Satan filled your heart *to lie to the Holy Spirit* and keep back part of the price of the land for yourself? While it remained, was it not your own? And after it was sold, was it not in your own control? Why have you conceived this thing in your heart? *You have not lied to men but to God.*

In verse 9 Peter said to Sapphira, "How is it that you have agreed together *to test the Spirit of the Lord*?" Both of them died on the spot—a grim reminder of the seriousness of lying to the Holy Spirit.

Some people argue that Ananias and Sapphira were believers. However, in addition to the statements of Peter and the obvious consequences, verse 1 calls Ananias "a certain man" rather than "a certain disciple." Here is a clue as to his true spiritual state. Like so many churchmen of today, he professed to be a believer but his heart was not right before God.

4. *By failing to believe that Christ was doing His miracles by the power of the Spirit and accusing Him of doing them by the power of Satan.*

This is a direct attack against the Person of Jesus Christ our Lord. It is committed by unbelievers. It is called "blasphemy against the Spirit" and is unforgiveable, according to Matthew 12:31,32.

Attacks against Christ are forgivable (Matthew 12:32), but speaking against the Holy Spirit is not. Many Bible teachers assume that continual rejection of Jesus Christ is the sin of blasphemy against the Holy Spirit. That is possible, but the specific incident in the context of Matthew 12:22-37 deals with our Lord's ability to cast out demons. The Pharisees attributed His power to the work of Satan. Therefore the blasphemy probably applies to their accusation. In any case, it is most serious to sin against the Holy Spirit of God.

Unbelievers are not aware that they are sinning against the Holy Spirit, nor do they believe it. They simply don't care what the Bible teaches. But until they stop sinning against the Spirit, there is no hope for them. It is the Holy Spirit who causes them to be born again and receive eternal life from God.

Hindering the Work of the Spirit

Believers can often ignore the ministry and work of the Holy Spirit. They hear of wild and fanciful interpretations of how the Holy Spirit works, and they want nothing to do with this. But the Holy Spirit is God! He lives inside the body of every believer (1 Corinthians 6:19), and He is our greatest resource, along with the Bible, for living the Christian life. We cannot afford to neglect or ignore His presence and power.

John was always suspicious of any sermon on the Holy Spirit. Whenever I referred to His work, John would accuse me of becoming charismatic! (All believers are charismatic, regardless of our views about the Holy Spirit's work.) One day I asked him if he believed that the Holy Spirit was living inside his body. He said that he did. I then asked him what he believed was the purpose of the Holy Spirit's presence in his life. He got a little nervous. He told me that he didn't want to have anything to do with pentecostal beliefs and practices. But I never said anything about such things.

After further discussions with John, he told me about his background. He had become disillusioned early in his Christian experience and had been deeply hurt. He was pressured to speak in tongues but simply could not do it. This led to further feelings of rejection and bitterness. Now he was hesitant to discuss anything about the Holy Spirit. How sad!

Fortunately for John, he became aware of his need of the Holy Spirit's ministry in his life and was able to talk about it without putting up a wall of resistance.

1. *Lusting against the Holy Spirit.*

Galatians 5:16,17 speak about this hindrance to the Holy Spirit's work which believers commit:

> I say then: Walk in the Spirit, and you shall not fulfill the lust of the flesh. For the flesh lusts against the Spirit, and the Spirit against the flesh; and these are contrary to one another, so that you do not do the things that you wish.

The "flesh" represents our sinful tendencies. These wrong desires are fighting against the Holy Spirit. There is a battle that goes on inside the believer between his old nature ("the flesh") and his new nature ("the spirit").

After explaining in a sermon the sinful nature of believers, a man confronted me afterward and said that I was wrong: True believers no longer have a sin nature; it is eradicated when you come to Christ. Since that had not proved true in my dealings with others or myself, nor did it coincide with my theology, I found it hard to accept what he said. I immediately turned to 1 John 1:8 and read these words to him:

> If we say that we have no sin, we deceive ourselves, and the truth is not in us.

He replied, "There must be another interpretation!" I had him read it again. He said, "It looks like you're right, but I find it hard to believe." His wife was standing nearby and responded, "Believe it, Harry—I've seen it!" Enough said!

Jesus said in Mark 7:21-23 that our sinful desires come from within our hearts and defile us. The problem is not with our environment and the many temptations we inevitably face each day—the problem is in our hearts! We are constantly fighting the Holy Spirit because our sinful desires want to control us rather than the Spirit's power. That's why we get so easily defeated in our Christian experience.

Paul wrote in Romans 7 about this struggle. He said

that the things we want to do that are good and right we don't do, and the things we want to avoid that are wrong we wind up doing. Such a dilemma! The only way to victory is through the work and ministry of the Holy Spirit, which is beautifully described in Romans 8.

Fighting the Spirit

Are you fighting against the Holy Spirit? No believer wants to believe he is. But I'm afraid this is often the case. It's hard to admit that the struggle goes on and that we need help. Our spiritual pride stands in the way, and as a result we remain frustrated and defeated most of the time. Our minds are captured by wrong ideas and thoughts. We desperately need the Spirit's help. Galatians 5:16 says that we must take a step at a time. We must "walk in the Spirit." This means to obey what the Spirit says in the Bible. Our sinful desires encourage us to do the opposite, and this wars against the Spirit. We must give up the battle and surrender to the will of the Spirit as revealed in the Bible. Until we do, we will have very little peace and victory.

2. Rejecting the Holy Spirit.

It seems incredible that believers could reject the Holy Spirit, but that is what 1 Thessalonians 4:1-8 teaches. The central problem of this passage deals with sexual immorality. Christians are warned about its consequences. If we reject this teaching about sexual purity, says verse 8, we are not rejecting man, but "God, who has also given us His Holy Spirit." The Spirit is often called the *Holy* Spirit, reminding us of His moral purity.

What a terrible conflict rages inside the believer's heart who is indwelt by the *Holy* Spirit but commits *unholy* acts! To "reject" means to set aside. We are trying to do away with what has been laid down as a law or principle of God. That's what our society does. It rejects the laws of God regarding sexual impurity. It has decided that individual freedom argues for sexual exploitation and self-gratification. But God's laws have not changed. Nothing so hinders the work of the Holy Spirit in our lives as committing acts of sexual immorality. The Spirit is hindered, and the emotional turmoil that results is simply an evidence of the terrible struggle that goes on inside our hearts.

Bob and Sue were Christians and married . . . but to other partners. Their love relationship was an affair, and though it was pleasurable to both of them, it was tearing them up emotionally. They hated the constant hiding. They both feared the day that their partners would discover their illicit relationship. Yet they often justified what they were doing. They spoke about how God had brought them together and that as long as they were not hurting anyone else, what harm could there be? They forgot one Person whom they were deeply offending—the Holy Spirit!

They still care about each other, but their Christian maturity was reflected in the decision they made—no more sex, period! They realized that what they were doing was wrong and was hindering the precious ministry of the Holy Spirit in their lives.

Sexual Immorality

You may call it something else, but *sexual immorality* is what God calls any sexual relationship outside the marital bond. It is wrong, and if you have been a believer for any length of time, you know it must stop! Until you make that decision and stop doing it, the Spirit's power will not be manifested in your life, no matter what you tell other believers. Stop kidding yourself and get right with God! A new power will fill your life, with new levels of peace, joy, and love.

3. *Grieving the Holy Spirit.*

Ephesians 4:30 says, "Do not grieve the Holy Spirit of God, by whom you were sealed for the day of redemption." The verses preceding this verse and following it deal with our attitudes and words. The way we react to other people has a serious effect upon the Holy Spirit of God, who lives inside us. The following sinful attitudes and responses are mentioned in Ephesians 4:25-31:

Lying
Anger
Stealing
Corrupt communication
Bitterness
Wrath
Clamor
Evil speaking
Malice

Not a very pleasant list, is it? Reading this list produces a sense of guilt in many of our hearts because these attitudes and responses are often inside us. When we do these things we are grieving the Holy Spirit— emotionally hurting a dear Friend who lives inside us.

In the case of anger, verse 27 says that it gives the devil an opportunity or a base of operations to do further damage in or through us. There is a time to be angry and a just cause over which to have anger. However, most of us get angry at people rather than issues. Our anger causes great grief to the Holy Spirit, who wants to pour out His love in our hearts (Romans 5:5).

Bill got into the habit of lying. As we all know, it is an easy habit to develop—it comes naturally. In his case he was trying to make himself look good. He started to believe these lies, and it became a serious problem in his Christian life. He even lied about being Spirit-filled.

He convinced other Christians that he was really walking with the Lord when in fact he had little personal relationship with God and spent little time in prayer. He made other people believe that he was a real prayer warrior and that he was reading his Bible in every spare moment of his life!

When Bill was challenged one day about his claims, he lost control, and his whole world fell in pieces. The truth was now out, and he was thoroughly embarrassed and humiliated in the eyes of his friends. All during this time he had trouble sleeping and was emotionally upset. He was not surprised when I told him that the trouble was caused because he was grieving the Holy Spirit. The turmoil was strong evidence that he was a believer. When there is no emotional upheaval inside a person, I wonder whether he really knows the Lord. Believers have a difficult time sinning against the Holy Spirit. There's a war going on inside.

4. *Quenching the Holy Spirit.*

To quench means to throw water on a fire. The Holy Spirit is like a fire inside us, but we can quench His power by what we say and do.

First Thessalonians 5 contains some short statements to believers that summarize Christian life and experience. Consider the following from verses 12-22:

> Recognize and esteem leaders.
> Be at peace.
> Warn the unruly.
> Comfort the fainthearted.
> Uphold the weak.
> Be patient with all.
> Don't seek revenge but pursue the good.
> Rejoice always.
> Pray without ceasing.